Discipleship The Way Jesus Did It

The Circle

CHOOSING *to* LEARN *from* LIFE

LEADER'S GUIDE

MIKE BREEN

NexGen® is an imprint of
Cook Communications Ministries, Colorado Springs, CO 80918
Cook Communications, Paris, Ontario
Kingsway Communications, Eastbourne, England

CHOOSING TO LEARN FROM LIFE LEADER'S GUIDE

First printing 2006
Printed in South Korea
1 2 3 4 5 6 7 8 9 10 Printing/Year 10 09 08 07 06 05

Cover Design: Brand Navigation, LLC

Mike Breen is the creator and developer of the LifeShapes material (formerly called LifeSkills) and the eight (8) shapes as a memorable method of discipleship.

ISBN: 0-78144-297-4

DVD CONTENTS   **RUNNING TIME**

"I can't believe I did that—again!"

Maybe you say that after getting another parking ticket. Maybe you say it after forgetting an important appointment or when you used a tone of voice with your children that you vowed you would never use again.

Or maybe you're asking, "What was that all about?" when an unexpected circumstance leaves you with more questions than answers.

We all have these moments. The Learning Circle helps us make sense of them. This study of *Choosing to Learn from Life* will not give formula answers so that your group members never make another mistake.

But it will give them the tools to recognize significant moments and learn from them in intentional ways. Understanding the Learning Circle will prepare you and your group to make the most of the lessons God wants you to learn.

WHY LIFESHAPES?

LifeShapes takes advantage of our tendency to remember what we see longer than we remember what we hear. Biblical principles connected to basic shapes help you remember how to follow Jesus' example in every aspect of your life. With these eight shapes, beginning with the Circle, you can learn to live as Jesus' disciple:

- **Circle:** Choosing to Learn from Life
- **Semi-circle:** Living in Rhythm with Life
- **Triangle:** Balancing the Relationships of Life
- **Square:** Defining the Priorities of Life
- **Pentagon:** Knowing Your Role in Life
- **Hexagon:** Praying as a Way of Life
- **Heptagon:** Practicing the Principles of a Vital Life
- **Octagon:** Living a Life with a Mission

These eight aspects of kingdom life are easy enough to show using simple shapes, yet deep enough that we will never reach the end of learning even one of them.

WHY A GROUP STUDY?

Community is at the heart of *LifeShapes* discipleship because it is the way Jesus did it. As you meet together, your group will have an opportunity to be vulnerable, and we encourage you to foster this kind of openness and honesty in your group through your own example. Be prepared to share your own reflections and answers to the questions in each session, and allow ample time for others to respond. By creating a safe setting where you and your group can own up to weak areas of your life, you can encourage each other in areas of strength and ministry. You can keep each other accountable to carry out personal challenges. You'll discover together a new perspective on following Jesus by looking at how Jesus lived out the Circle all around the shores and villages of Galilee.

YOUR TOOLS

Several tools are available to enrich your study, and you can choose the combination that will work best for your group. If you began your study of *LifeShapes* with *A Passionate Life Small Group Resource*, you will recognize that we have retained the same structure and format in this Leader's Guide so that you can make a seamless transition in your teaching.

- *Choosing to Learn from Life Leader's Guide* provides a step-by-step lesson to follow. In addition to the discussion questions in the participant workbook, the leader's guide offers further discussion questions to use at your discretion.

- *Choosing to Learn from Life Workbook* provides a place for group participants to discuss and record their reactions and insights, as well as to take notes on the principles of each shape.

- *Choosing to Learn from Life Teaching DVD* provides video segments of Mike Breen, creator of *LifeShapes*, giving an in depth presentation of the Learning Circle. Using the DVD requires a DVD player and television or a DVD drive in your computer. To access the enhanced portion of your DVD, you will need to have a computer with a DVD-Rom drive, Microsoft® PowerPoint® or QuickTime® Version 6 or better.

- The *Choosing to Learn from Life* PowerPoint® presentation (QuickTime® movie also provided for those without PowerPoint®), also found on the DVD, provides slides you can use as you go through the Learning Circle with your group. Throughout the study, your Leader's Guide will show you a reduction of the corresponding slide from the PowerPoint® presentation.

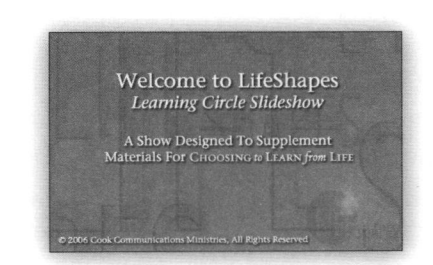

- If you purchased the small group resource kit, you have been given a copy of the book ***Choosing to Learn from Life.*** Although this study can be done effectively without the book, we highly recommend that everyone in the group have a copy to read. As a leader or group facilitator you will find a wealth of additional material in it that will help you in your own discipleship and with the study.

Throughout this year, more resources will become available to you for in-depth study of each of the *LifeShapes*. Visit **www.LifeShapes.com** for more information and future release dates.

USING THIS LEADER'S GUIDE

You can probably suggest other variables that affect your group in unique ways. Whatever your setting and group characteristics, following a basic structure each week will help you make the most of your time together. Each session is organized around three concepts: Reflect, Respond, and React.

Reflect

As you begin each session, take some time for participants to share their real-life reactions to the concepts you studied in the previous session. Then use the opening material in the participant workbook to introduce the theme behind the new session. The participant workbook offers several discussion questions at this stage. This process will help you shape your leadership of the next segment.

Respond

In this section you'll get into the presentation and discussion of each new concept. This leader's guide includes some additional teaching text for each session, along with discussion questions. In this part of your time together, everyone has an opportunity to see and discuss the detailed principles and applications of the Learning Circle.

The questions in the workbook marked by the "Huddles" icon allow participants to break up into smaller groups for discussion. In addition to "Huddles," you'll find "Going Deeper" questions mixed in with or at the end of each Respond section. These will allow for meaningful group discussion before presenting the week's homework. Choose how many of these questions to use based on your timeframe and group members.

React

In this section, you'll find material that turns the discussion from the general to the specific—getting more personal. Members will consider how the concepts you're studying affect their individual paths of discipleship. Encourage participants to use the space provided for writing a personal response. They will have an opportunity to accept a personal challenge for how they will apply the concepts of each session during the coming week.

As your group gets to know each other and grows closer during the sessions together, members may begin to feel comfortable sharing these personal challenges with each other and helping each other become accountable for these challenges. Remember, the goal is to develop a community where these principles are not only taught but lived out together.

Close your time together with prayer. Ask for God's insight into understanding the phases of the Learning Circle and guidance in applying it.

A PASSIONATE LIFE

As you go through life, you undoubtedly come to these significant moments where you simply have to stop and ask yourself: Is this all there is for me? You know you want more; you want to serve God, you want to serve others. You want to love others the way you're truly supposed to, and when it is all over, you want to leave behind a legacy of your walk on this earth. You want to be remembered for your love and your passion, but so often, you just can't figure out what that looks like in tangible terms. You're passionate about something that you care about deeply, something that stirs deep emotions in you, something that you feel right to your core. How do you live a life where all of your hopes, dreams, and passions are fully realized? Take a look at the life of Jesus, he lived out his passions, and he taught others to do the same. He is the perfect example that you can turn to when you find yourself at life's standstill asking these very questions. Jesus calls us to join him in the practice of passionate discipleship.

A passionate walk with Jesus.

A passionate faith that spills over into everything you do.

A passionate energy for the kingdom of God.

A passionate conviction to minister to the needs around you.

A passionate search for others ready to meet Jesus.

A PASSIONATE LIFE.

1 "LEARN FROM ME"

D o you ever have moments when someone is looking up to you and you suddenly feel the enormous pressure to have all the answers? But you don't, and you know you don't. You're just not sure you want anyone else to find out. Let your guard down. We're all learners, no matter what stage of discipleship we're in. Let your group know it's okay to admit to struggles. This study is based on the dynamics of community and transparency, so take the opportunity to foster openness and honesty at the very beginning so that the community of faith can bind together in support of everyone.

IN THIS SESSION, YOUR GROUP WILL:

Learn that Jesus really is the answer to life's challenges

•

Explore the different ways we try to live a fulfilling life

•

Discover the refreshment that comes from living in God's kingdom

•

Form a plan to carry the right tools for a meaningful spiritual life

PREPARATION:

- Read the Introduction and Chapter 1 from *Choosing to Learn from Life.*
- Read Matthew 11:28–30.
- If you are using *Choosing to Learn from Life Teaching DVD,* set up your equipment.
- Make sure you have a Bible to use in your session.
- Answer the discussion questions yourself so that you will have material for examples or prompting.

SCRIPTURAL BASIS:

- **Matthew 11:28–30** — When Jesus says, "Take my yoke upon you…" we tend to think he is asking us to exchange our burdens for his. A yoke is not a burden; rather, it is a way of sharing the weight of a burden. So, what Jesus is saying in this verse is, "Let's share life together, and in the process, let me teach you how to live in a way that brings rest to your soul."

IF **THIS IS YOUR FIRST TIME** meeting together, take a few minutes to get acquainted before beginning your session with worship, prayer, or an icebreaker. Then allow a few minutes for participants to review pages 9-10 and answer the "Thinking Ahead" questions.

Take time to briefly highlight the main idea of *LifeShapes*. We live in a visual society and remember what we see more than what we hear. The Learning Circle is designed to provide a visual reminder of important discipleship principles. Ask a volunteer to read aloud "In Good Company" from the participant workbook, page 11.

The best way to begin this study is to emphasize the importance of community. The Circle is designed around Jesus' example of living in community with his disciples which facilitated an environment of discussion and accountability. Encourage your participants

IN GOOD COMPANY

THE **FILM** *In Good Company* (starring Topher Grace) tells the story of Carter Duryea. Duryea is a 26 year-old whiz kid of a multinational conglomerate, GLOBECOM. He is promoted to the head of the ad sales department of *Sports America Magazine*, GLOBECOM's latest acquisition. To complicate the plot, this business success coincides with the disintegration of his marriage. Duryea is being groomed for greatness at GLOBECOM. He's under pressure to produce big things. In reality he is lonely, insecure, and unprepared for life. His ideas and decisions cause conflict with the *Sports America* team.

At the close of the film Duryea loses his position and decides to start over. But before he leaves, he makes a profound admission to his colleague, Dan Foreman (played by Dennis Quaid). He thanks Foreman and says that no one had ever cared enough to give him a hard time before or to teach him the things that he really needed to know about life.[1]

In fact, the entire film is about change. It serves as an extraordinary example of how mankind is so often unwilling to accept or implement change in life. Then, when faced with the consequences of those decisions, such as a

crumbling marriage or unclear career path, we are forced to make clear-cut decisions, change or don't change. Carter Duryea spends most of his time promising change but resisting true transformation. He deals with all kinds of significant moments in which he is presented with an opportunity to change. In the end, he finally learns that his own personal happiness and fruitfulness as a human being depends on his ability to learn and grow from the challenges he faces.

—from ***Choosing to Learn from Life***, Chapter 1

[1] Paul Weitz, *In Good Company*, DVD, directed by Paul Weitz (Hollywood, CA: Universal, 2004).

11

to make an effort in the beginning to open up to each other and share honest thoughts and feelings regarding the material.

The questions on page 12 of the participant workbook are designed to break the ice and begin conversation among the group. Ask the group to share their answers to these questions. You may choose to discuss the questions as a whole group or have the participants break into smaller groups of 2 or 3 to discuss some or all of the questions.

Take a few minutes to answer the following questions:

◯ When is a time your life felt out of control?

◯ How well-equipped do you feel for dealing with the challenges of your life as it is today? Explain.

◯ Is there a person in your life who isn't afraid to challenge you in areas of your life that may be questionable? Describe your relationship with this person.

12

● ●

 IF YOU ARE using the DVD as part of your study, watch Chapter 1 now. Mike Breen tells the story of the Sun Shower. If you are not using the DVD, read the abbreviated version that appears here.

THE SUN SHOWER

I was relaxing in the hot tub at the health club when my daughters came up to me and asked if I had tried the Sun Shower yet.

"I don't even know what a Sun Shower is," I admitted.

They pointed. "It's that white tube over by the pool. You stand up in it and get a tan, but you also get totally refreshed. It's like standing on the beach in South Carolina."

In my opinion the beaches of South Carolina are the closest things to perfection that you can find here on earth. "What does it take?" I asked.

"A pound for three minutes."

So I rummaged for a one-pound coin and walked over to the Sun Shower. The door opened to a room the size of a small closet. Nothing looked too dangerous, so I stepped in and closed the door. Still not certain of what I was doing, I made sure to read the instructions clear through. Following them carefully, I put on a pair of goggles that was hanging in there and shut my eyes tightly. Nothing happened.

Of course. The one-pound coin.

I opened my eyes, took off the goggles, put the coin in the slot, pulled the goggles back on, and waited. Nothing. This in no way resembled the beach in South Carolina.

When the three minutes were up, I stepped out. "What did you think?" my daughters asked.

They looked so excited. Clearly they thought the Sun Shower was a fantastic idea. But I had to be honest.

"Well," I said, "I guess I just don't get it. I mean, it was okay, but probably something you girls would like better."

Elizabeth and Rebecca were profoundly disappointed. They had wanted so badly for me to share their experience, and I hadn't. Frankly, I thought the whole thing was rather strange, but I didn't say much about it.

The next week we were back at the health club. Rebecca and Elizabeth came up to me with renewed fervor.

"Dad," they said, "this time try it for six minutes. Maybe three minutes wasn't enough for you to start feeling the effects. Give it six minutes, okay?"

So back I went to the white tube. I stepped inside the room, pulled the door closed, read the instructions, put on the goggles, and squeezed my eyes shut. Nothing.

Oh, right. The coins. Goggles off, coins in, goggles on. I closed my eyes again and waited. Six minutes is a long time to wait when you're standing in an enclosed booth with your eyes shut, listening to whirring and clicking noises. When it was over, I took off the goggles and hung them back on the hook and left.

Elizabeth and Rebecca were anxiously waiting for me. "How was it this time, Dad? Did you feel the effects this time?"

I looked at my daughters' expectant faces. "I don't really think it's for me."

They thought I was completely daft.

"This is something for you and your friends to enjoy," I said. "Maybe I'm just too old to get the full benefits of it."

One thing I must say for my children: they don't give up easily. The next week they were ready.

"Dad, try it this time for nine minutes. You'll really love it if you give it enough time. C'mon, Dad!"

So I went in the tube, pulled the door shut, and read the instructions for the third time. They hadn't changed a word. I put on the goggles and closed my eyes.

Sigh. The coins.

Goggles off, coins in, goggles on, eyes closed. Let me tell you, if six minutes is a long time, then nine minutes is a very long time to stand in a closet in the dark listening to clicks and whirrs. So I took a chance and opened my eyes—only to find that I could see right through the goggles. Looking around, I wondered if I would get more of a tan if I stood closer to the mirror.

Then I saw some things that looked like coat hooks on the wall. Mmm. I thought that maybe they were there to reflect the rays. Standing still for nine minutes was not much more interesting than keeping my eyes closed for nine minutes, so I turned around.

I saw a doorknob. What was this? I turned the knob, and the door opened to a room filled with the most refreshing light rays and replicated ocean breeze I could ever imagine.

For three weeks I had been standing in the changing room.

—from *A Passionate Life*,
Introduction

After the story, discuss these questions as a group:

☞ In what ways are we like Mike, standing outside of where the real joy is in our spiritual lives? (*We're not sure what to do or where to go because it's something different.*)

☞ What keeps us from opening the door and entering the full joy of knowing Jesus? (*Uncertainty about what will happen; being comfortable with the way things are; resistance to dealing with a sin issue.*)

You can supplement the DVD segment or story with the following material, or use this material independently. Be sure to allow time for Huddles to discuss the questions in the participant workbook and Going Deeper questions as appropriate.

→HUDDLES←

Whenever you see the "Huddles" icon, have your group break up into Huddles (groups of 2 or 3). Read the following paragraphs aloud; then give the Huddles a few minutes to discuss each question before moving on to the Going Deeper discussion questions. Your group may stay in their Huddles while you present material from each section.

All you have to do is pick up a couple of books or watch television to get a picture of our culture's quest to be better and better. "Reality shows" point out the desperate search for meaning and happiness. People go on these shows to be better dressers, better spouses, better parents, or richer people.

We soon see that we are not isolated in our desire to learn how to live our lives to the fullest. Some of us, though, don't try to get fixed. Instead we want to escape. We watch sports on TV, remembering our high school or college days. Or we engage in the world of computer games. It's a world away from a life that we can do nothing about and where circumstances never seem to change.

→HUDDLES← ➲ When you run into tough or challenging situations, do you intentionally look for quick ways to "get fixed" or to completely escape? Why do you think this is? ➲

We Christians go to our churches and Bible studies looking for answers. "Jesus is the answer." With our heads, we believe that. Experientially, it's a different story. What does that mean on a day-to-day basis? How is Jesus the answer when you can't keep up with your bills no matter how hard you work? How is Jesus the answer when your best friend betrays you? How is Jesus the answer when a difficult child frays at the garment of your family life? The question is not one of knowledge but of application. But we can't admit that, can we? We can't let the people

GOING DEEPER:

➲ Why is it sometimes easier to escape than to deal with a problem head-on? *(We don't like confrontation. We don't want to admit being wrong. We don't know what the outcome will be.)*

➲ Why can't someone on the outside "fix" you? *(You have to admit your own problems. Nothing will change until you are ready to change. No one can really make you do something you don't want to.)*

around us—especially other Christians—know that we haven't figured out how to apply the only true answer. So we carry on, wondering, frustrated, disappointed, and living in the shadow of the passionate life that Jesus offers but that we have rarely experienced.

This, however, is far from doing life as God designed it. He made us to be authentic with each other. But what does authenticity look like? It means that we are honest with each other—we are open with the sharing of our thoughts and feelings. It also means that we must sometimes boldly take the initiative in sharing ourselves with others. Likewise, we must also learn empathy if we are to be authentic. We have to know how to understand and react appropriately to the thoughts and feelings of others. This is how God created us to do life together.

HUDDLES ◉ Evaluate how authentic you are with the people around you? Explain. ◉

Being a Christian doesn't necessarily mean you've got life all figured out. And it doesn't mean that you live life perfectly. Trying to do that will just get you tired. There is good news! Listen to these words from Jesus. Ask someone to read Matthew 11:28–30 aloud.

GOING DEEPER:

◉ Sometimes, in our desire to project a certain image to other people, we end up not being ourselves. What kind of "false" image do you project? Why is this? *(We don't want to appear weak. We want people to think we're in control of our lives. We are afraid of losing our privacy.)*

"Come to me, all you who are weary and burdened, and I will give you rest. Take my yoke upon you and learn from me, for I am gentle and humble in heart, and you will find rest for your souls. For my yoke is easy and my burden is light."

—Matthew 11:28–30

The One whom we know to be The Answer offers us an invitation. "Learn from me." When we're tired of the ruts that we are stuck in and the inability to make decisions and work through circumstances of life, we have hope: Learn from Jesus. Is there any better teacher? We spend a lot of time reading books and listening to CDs that claim to have the power to transform our lives. But how do we know which ones will work best for us, or even if the teachings are biblically sound? We tend to forget that, buried beneath all the books and resources of our collection, lies the one and only teacher who can show us everything we need: Jesus.

→HUDDLES← ⊘ Write down or discuss your personal interpretation of Matthew 11:28-30. ⊘

GOING DEEPER:

⊘ Why do we sometimes hesitate to take Jesus up on the offer he makes in Matthew 11:28–30?

19

ASK SOMEONE TO read "Check Your Tool Belt" aloud from the participant workbook (page 16). Or, allow some quiet time for group members to read silently. Then discuss these questions:

◉ Sometimes we try to make do with a tool that is not quite right. What usually happens to the project when we do that?

◉ When life's problems are so big, do you ever feel there's simply no tool available that could fix the issue you're dealing with? What do you do in those situations?

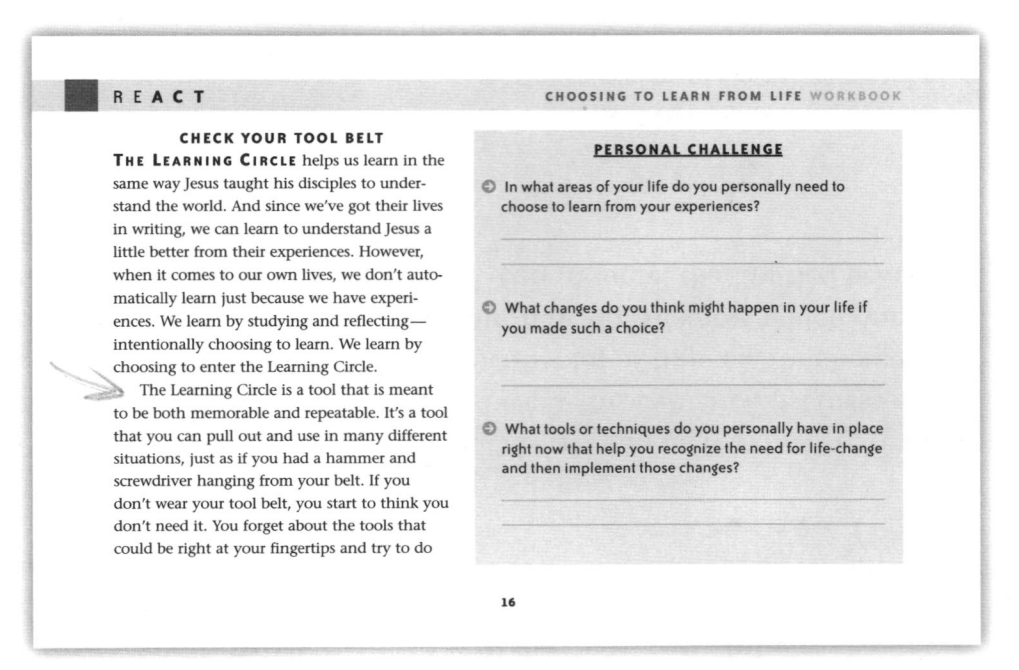

R E A CT   CHOOSING TO LEARN FROM LIFE WORKBOOK

CHECK YOUR TOOL BELT
THE LEARNING CIRCLE helps us learn in the same way Jesus taught his disciples to understand the world. And since we've got their lives in writing, we can learn to understand Jesus a little better from their experiences. However, when it comes to our own lives, we don't automatically learn just because we have experiences. We learn by studying and reflecting—intentionally choosing to learn. We learn by choosing to enter the Learning Circle.

The Learning Circle is a tool that is meant to be both memorable and repeatable. It's a tool that you can pull out and use in many different situations, just as if you had a hammer and screwdriver hanging from your belt. If you don't wear your tool belt, you start to think you don't need it. You forget about the tools that could be right at your fingertips and try to do

PERSONAL CHALLENGE

◉ In what areas of your life do you personally need to choose to learn from your experiences?

◉ What changes do you think might happen in your life if you made such a choice?

◉ What tools or techniques do you personally have in place right now that help you recognize the need for life-change and then implement those changes?

16

As you wrap up your session, point out the Personal Challenge questions on pages 16-17 in the participant workbook. Allow some quiet time for individuals to write personal answers. Ask members to share the personal challenges they have set for themselves with at least one other person in the group. Encourage participants to prepare for the next session by answering the "Thinking Ahead" questions at the beginning of Session 2, page 20.

Discuss how to support each other's plans for implementing these changes. Close your session with prayer.

---

things the hard way—and probably hurt yourself in the process!

All too often we only go halfway around the Circle, then we forget about the rest of the tools we have available to complete the job. God wants us to be a completed project—not something left unfinished. He will continue to produce events in our lives that seem to us the same lesson over and over again. Only when we make it through the entire Circle do we begin to see life changing results.

Be ready to share in the next session about your experiences of choosing to learn this week.

PERSONAL CHALLENGE

◐ Which part of the Circle is hardest for you to go through? Why?

_____

_____

_____

_____

_____

17

2 WHEN TIME STANDS STILL

Are your days usually filled with so many errands, activities, and events that you can barely seem to keep up with life's screaming pace? There never seems to be enough time in the day to get everything accomplished. Living like Jesus isn't about finding more time in your day—it's about making the most of the time you have. Have you ever experienced an event, a moment that stopped you in your tracks, a moment when nothing else mattered? That instant in time seems to swallow up everything around it, and you realize that something just happened that is going to change your life. Your natural instinct might be to fight the change, especially if the event is a negative or painful one. Jesus shows you how to welcome those moments and use them to learn how to live in his kingdom.

IN THIS SESSION, YOUR GROUP WILL:

Define and learn to recognize *kairos* moments

•

Explore the process of learning from *kairos* moments

•

Discover how to see God's kingdom at work in *kairos* moments

•

Form a plan to welcome an individual *kairos* moment

PREPARATION:

- Read Chapter 2 from *Choosing to Learn from Life.*
- Read Mark 1:14–15.
- If you are using *Choosing to Learn from Life Teaching DVD* or the *Learning Circle Slideshow* presentation, set up your equipment.
- Make sure you have Bibles to use in your session.
- Answer the discussion questions yourself so that you will have material for examples or prompting.

SCRIPTURAL BASIS:

- **Mark 1:15** — "The time has come," Jesus says. The time for what? This is no ordinary revelation like "time for lunch," or "time to take out the trash." This is Jesus telling us that God is here. The time that God shall come down from his kingdom to live among men is no longer an idea of the future, it is right now. And for us to experience life with God, both now and in the future, Jesus gives the greatest instruction on how to live life in the presence of God: repent and believe.

KEY WORDS:

Kairos

●

Time

●

Kingdom

●

Repent

●

Believe

WELCOME YOUR GROUP members. As they come in, encourage them to review the pages 19-20 of Session 2 and answer the "Thinking Ahead" questions.

Begin with a brief review of Session 1. Invite participants to share some of their personal challenges during the week. This would be a great opportunity for you to mentally collect a database of personal *kairos* events for the people in your group. You can use these events throughout the study to help people walk through the steps of the Circle and learn from the event. Having a collection of events from the people in your group will allow for more personal

---

OUT OF CONTROL

DO YOU EVER feel as if you're living on a merry-go-round? That life is happening to you, and it's going by so fast you don't know what to focus on? Life is a challenge. Every day we have the same number of minutes and hours of time. Some of those moments may actually be beyond our control, and we have to step back and admit that. But they're never beyond God's control.

As a follower and friend of Jesus, you want your life to count—to have a purpose and meaning. The world offers material gain,

temporary success, and fleeting recognition, but that's just not enough. You desire to leave a legacy where all that you did in this world, whether in your career, your family life, or your ministry, makes a difference in the eternal lives of other people. That is living in the kingdom of God which is a whole different story.

Living in the kingdom is not a fleeting experience. It lasts forever. At the very beginning of his ministry, Jesus tells of a great opportunity: God's kingdom is within our reach. Jesus tells us just what we

have to do: go through a process of repentance and belief. The process can be challenging—even painful. But through this process we learn how to follow Jesus into the kingdom. That's when life starts to make sense.

—from *A Passionate Life*,
Chapter 3

21

---

examples and experiences than you will get from simply pulling from these resource materials. Pray

for continued openness to learning from Jesus.

Then ask a volunteer to read aloud "Out of Control" in the participant workbook (page 21).

The questions on page 22 of the participant workbook are designed to break the ice and begin conversation among the group. Ask the group to share answers to these discussion questions.

Encourage participants to take the discussion out of the realm of the theoretical and into the personal. Vulnerability and trust are essential to building authentic community, but both take time and effort.

You may discuss only some questions as a group and encourage participants to explore the other questions on their own time.

Take a few minutes to answer the following questions:

⊜ Reflect on the larger periods of time or seasons in your life. During which stages did you feel the most significance in your life? Why?

⊜ What do you think determines whether your life has purpose or meaning?

⊜ What is one aspect of your life that outwardly shows that you belong to the kingdom of God?

22

→DVD←

IF YOU ARE using the DVD as part of your study, watch Chapter 2 now. Point out the fill-in-the-blank sections in the participant workbook and remind group members to watch for key words. After watching the segment, discuss these questions as a group:

➲ What made Mike's experience with his son a *kairos* moment? *(It was an experience that challenged him to change. It was something that mattered more than anything else around.)*

➲ Why do you think painful times are often *kairos* times? *(Because we want the pain to stop, we really look at the experience to see what we could change.)*

R E S P O N D   CHOOSING TO LEARN FROM LIFE WORKBOOK

AS YOU LEARN about *kairos* moments together with your group, fill in key words in the sections that follow.

Jesus broke into actual human history. He is not a theoretical religious figure. He walked the roads of Galilee and Judea at a specific point in time, and time has never been the same since then. Jesus began his ministry with a very short sermon—a sermon that is the summary statement of all his teaching and ideas for the coming few years. This message sets the stage for all he is about to say and do.

> *After John was put in prison, Jesus went into Galilee, proclaiming the good news of God.*
> *"The time has come," he said. "The kingdom of God is near. Repent and believe the good news!"*
> —*Mark 1:14–15*

In these sentences we discover how Jesus helped his disciples understand the world and to learn from their experiences. These two verses fix Jesus in chronological time—after John was put in prison—and summarize his message—the message that is at the heart of the Learning Circle. Let's take the time to dig a little deeper to really understand what Jesus is saying to us.

Mark 1:15 contains four key words for the Learning Circle:

1. _____
2. _____
3. _____
4. _____

23

---

*You can supplement the DVD segment with the following material, or use this material independently to explain the concepts of kairos moments. Be sure to allow time to discuss the questions in the participant workbook and Going Deeper questions as appropriate. You can find a fuller discussion of kairos moments in Chapter 3 of **Choosing to Learn from Life**.*

→HUDDLES←

Whenever you see the "Huddles" icon, have your group break into Huddles of 2 or 3. Read the following paragraphs aloud; then give the Huddles a few minutes to discuss each question. Your group may stay in their Huddles while you present material from each section.

(Prepare Slides 2-13). Display Slide 2. **Jesus broke into actual human history. He is not a theoretical religious figure. He walked the roads of Galilee and Judea at a specific point in time, and time has never been the same since then.**

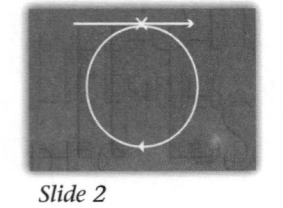

Slide 2

Galilee was known to have incredibly fertile land, greater than anywhere else in Palestine. Surrounded by Gentiles, Galilee's history was one of constant struggle as surrounding nations sought to dominate the area. By the time of Jesus, Galilee's great roads led out all over the known world. It wasn't a large area, but it overflowed with people. Galilee was a fertile ground for new ideas, the ideal place to share a new and radical message.

Display Slide 3. **Jesus begins his ministry with a very short sermon—a sermon that is the summary statement of all his teaching and ideas for the coming few years. This message sets the stage for all he is about to say and do.**
Display Slide 4 and Slide 5.

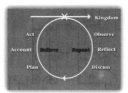

Slide 3

After John was put in prison, Jesus went into Galilee, proclaiming the good news of God. "The time has come," he said. "The kingdom of God is near. Repent and believe the good news!"

—Mark 1:14–15

In these sentences we discover how Jesus helped his disciples fully understand the world and to learn from their experiences. These two verses fix Jesus in time and summarize his message—the message that is at the heart of the Learning Circle. Let's take the time to dig a little deeper to really understand what Jesus is saying to us.

Slide 4

Slide 5

Mark 1:15 contains four key words for the Learning Circle. *Display Slide 6.*

1. <u>Time</u>. *Display Slide 7.*
2. <u>Kingdom</u>. *Display Slide 8.*
3. <u>Repent</u>. *Display Slide 9.*
4. <u>Believe</u>.

In English, we have the word "time" and we use it many different ways. Greek, the original language of the New Testament, has many words for time with specific meanings. The two most common are:

Chronos—meaning <u>wristwatch time</u>; and
Kairos—meaning <u>event time</u>.

Display Slide 10. Chronos is the kind of time that is sequential, calendar time, wristwatch time. *Chronos* is the kind of time we would use in the question: "What time is it?" or "What time are we eating dinner tonight?" It's the kind of time where you're conscious of the sequence of ongoing time, how long something takes, measured in minutes or hours.

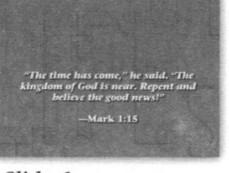

Slide 6

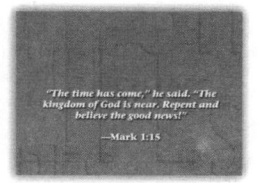

Slide 7

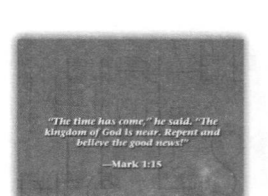

Slide 8

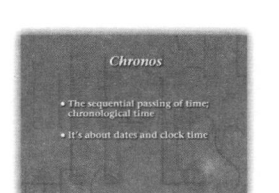

Slide 9

Slide 10

→HUDDLES← ➔ Write down your own example of *chronos* time. *(Any kind of ordinary event that goes by the clock.)* ➔

Display Slide 11. **Kairos** is completely different. **Kairos** is event time, crisis time, the kind of time that we would use in the statement, "That was a great time last night" or "Didn't we have a good time the other day?" "What a time that was!" You are not aware of the clock when it's *kairos* time. In that moment time seems to <u>stand still</u>.

Display Slide 12. **Kairos** is a period of time when **chronos** is of no importance.

Display Slide 13. **Kairos** marks a significant shift in your life.

→HUDDLES← ➔ Take a minute to think of some of the significant events that have taken place throughout your life.

1. _____
2. _____
3. _____

➔ How did these experiences affect your life after that point?

31

GOING DEEPER:

➔ What makes us mindful of the progress of the clock? *(Having appointments, being bored or uncomfortable, a long list of things to do.)*

➔ What makes us lose track of *chronos* time? *(An experience we really enjoy and are interested in. Something that happens suddenly that is more important than what we were doing.)*

Slide 11

Slide 12

Slide 13

These were *kairos* events. These were occasions when *chronos* time was of no importance. You weren't watching the clock because that's not the kind of time that mattered.

Kairos events can either be <u>positive</u> or <u>negative</u> experiences. They can be times of celebration and joy or times of pain and sadness. *Kairos* marks a significant <u>shift</u> in your life.

Think about the day you graduated from college or began a new job. You may not remember how long the ceremony was, but it was definitely an event when time stood still. *Kairos.*

Maybe you remember the day you got engaged or married. *Kairos.*

The promotion at work that changed the way your family lives. *Kairos.*

A death in the family changed your role and relationships. *Kairos.*

→HUDDLES←

➲ How would you recognize a *kairos* event in the future?

➲ Choose a *kairos* moment and tell how you responded to it and whether it was positive or negative. *(Answers will vary. Encourage people to express the emotions they felt at the time of the event and what decisions they had to make because of the event.)* ➲

GOING DEEPER:

* Why is it important to us to recognize *kairos* moments? Is there any difference between a big *kairos* event and a small one? *(When we recognize kairos moments, we can learn from them. Little ones have as much potential to teach us something as the big ones.)*

Jesus says to his listeners that they have a great opportunity. God's kingdom is within reach! However, taking hold of this amazing opportunity involves a process of repentance and belief.

Now to both the courageous Galileans and to us today, such an offer may seem exciting. But what exactly is Jesus talking about? What does he mean?

Some *kairos* events mark our lives because of the pain they bring: The death of a loved one—you remember when you heard the news and the words just hung in the air. Perhaps a relationship came to a screeching halt for another reason—break-up, divorce, or betrayal of friendship. Maybe you lost your job. In these instances time stood still, didn't it? That's one way of recognizing that you have entered *kairos* time: the event leaves an impact on you—and it's rarely neutral.

When we look for them, we realize *kairos* events take place everywhere! We go to a restaurant, and it's a terrific meal or a dismal stress. We're sitting at an intersection, and we look at the wrong set of lights. We think that they're green, we move and then we realize the mistake. We have a near miss on the freeway. We have an argument or a challenge in our lives, and it causes us some kind of crisis. We have great times, and we have awful times. It is most often our painful *kairos* moments that we choose to ignore because we want to avoid the pain of the experience. However, we often find that God is doing some of his most significant work in our lives during those painful times and so it becomes critically important not to ignore or attempt to escape those moments of hurt and heartache.

→HUDDLES← ◗ Think of a *kairos* moment that was particularly painful. Share how you were able to grow spiritually through that experience.

ASK SOMEONE TO read aloud "Everyday Opportunities" from the participant's workbook, page 27. Or, allow some quiet time for group members to read silently. Then discuss these questions as a group:

➲ In what parts of your ordinary day could you look for *kairos* moments?

➲ What is exciting about moving forward in your discipleship experience? What is a little scary about it for you?

EVERYDAY OPPORTUNITIES

SO WE LEARN to recognize *kairos* events. Now what? What do we do with them? We might be tempted to file them away in the back of our minds and ignore them, even forget them, especially if they have a negative effect. We may think through the events that led to the kairos moment so that we never find ourselves in that situation again. But when a *kairos* event has a positive effect, we want to draw it out as long as possible. We relive the moment again and again. We look at pictures or mementos and remember the feelings, the pleasure of the experience.

Kairos presents an opportunity. This takes God out of the boxes of our Sunday school classes, our Bible studies, and services where we may have stored him. God can and wants to impact every part of our lives. With every occasion in your life, whether a positive event or negative, Jesus gives you an opportunity to move forward in discipleship. It's a great opportunity for you to grow as a person; it's a

PERSONAL CHALLENGE

➲ Write down a *kairos* event you have experienced recently. How did you respond?

_____

_____

_____

➲ Looking back, how do you wish you had responded to your *kairos* moment?

_____

_____

_____

_____

27

As you wrap up your session, point out the "Personal Challenge" on pages 27-28 of the participant workbook. Allow some quiet time for individuals to write personal answers. Ask members to share the personal challenges that they have set for themselves with at least one other person in the group.

Encourage participants to prepare for the next session by answering the "Thinking Ahead" questions at the beginning of Session 3.

Discuss how to support each other's plans for implementing these changes. Close your session with prayer.

wonderful opportunity for you to step into the process of learning the way that Jesus teaches. It's an opportunity for God to intervene and for you to learn from Jesus.

The Lord wants each of us to learn how to make the most of each event. When we learn from these experiences, we enter the kingdom of God afresh. We receive anew what it means to grow in him.

Be ready to share in the next session about your *kairos* experiences this week.

○ Write down one specific area of your life where you would like the Lord to show you a *kairos* moment this week so you can learn from it.

_____

_____

_____

_____

_____

_____

28

3 THE RETURN OF THE KING

The kingdom of God. The Bible gives several descriptions of the kingdom that numb the mind with their magnificence. Yet, we can barely grasp how incredible it will truly be. Our future holds a place where there is no pain, no sickness, no sadness, no war, and no death. Yet, even now in the present, we experience moments where Jesus takes away our pain, heals our sicknesses, brings peace to our souls and to the earth, and raises the dead. Jesus shows us moments where the future kingdom breaks into the present, giving us a glimpse of the eternity we are destined for.

IN THIS SESSION, YOUR GROUP WILL:

Learn that the kingdom of God is present now

•

Explore the relationship between *kairos* and *kingdom*

•

Discover the role of repentance and faith in the process of learning

•

Form a plan to examine personal *kairos* moments

PREPARATION:

- Read Chapter 3 from *Choosing to Learn from Life*.
- Revelation 21:3–5 and Matthew 18:18–20.
- If you are using the *Choosing to Learn from Life Teaching DVD* or the *Learning Circle Slideshow* presentation, set up your equipment.
- Make sure you have Bibles to use in your session.
- Answer the discussion questions yourself so that you will have material for examples or prompting.

SCRIPTURAL BASIS:

KEY WORDS:

Kingdom
•
Repent
•
Believe
•
Disciple

- **Revelation 21:3-5** — The kingdom of God, a place this verse describes as being free from death, crying, sickness, and pain. It is often a place people think of as the future realm of heaven, and while that is true, Jesus taught that the kingdom of God is here, in the present. God the King lives within us, and wherever the King is present, so too is the kingdom. We get to experience daily moments where God reveals the same powers of the eternal kingdom to our lives in the present.

- **Matthew 28:18-20** — A disciple is not only a learner of that which is taught to him but also an imitator of the one who teaches him. Jesus made his followers into people who would imitate him in every aspect of their lives. His command therefore, was for his disciples to go out and imitate his life, to live as he lived. But Jesus didn't stop there. He gave the command that we are to create more followers that would also imitate him. Making people who genuinely imitate the life of Jesus is what the great commission is all about.

WELCOME YOUR GROUP members. As they come in, encourage them to review pages 29-30 of Session 3 and answer the "Thinking Ahead" questions. Ask them to use the questions and answers in conversation with others in the group before you get started.

Begin with a brief review of Session 2. Invite participants to share some of their own *kairos* moments during the past week and how they experienced the kingdom of God. Pray for continued understanding of the Circle.

Next, ask a volunteer to read aloud "How Did We Get Here?" from the participant workbook (page 31).

REFLECT   CHOOSING TO LEARN FROM LIFE WORKBOOK

HOW DID WE GET HERE?

A FOUR-YEAR OLD BOY finds a loaded gun under his parents' dresser. Bang! Bang! He shoots his two-year-old sibling.

In Israel, a nineteen-year-old man boards a bus knowing he won't get off. No one will. In a few minutes it blows up. The suicide bomber has lived out his destiny.

A fourteen-year-old girl goes missing from her family for more than a year, snatched against her will by cultish religious fanatics.

Four prisoners kill a guard and escape, armed and dangerous.

In Iraq, innocent children are maimed and killed by bombs set by their own people.

A CEO of a major corporation manipulates the books. He makes a fortune. Stockholders lose their retirement money.

This is the stuff of daily newscasts. We get a snack during the commercials and come back to hear the five-day weather forecast and the sports.

How did the world get to such a state that events like these are routine—and we barely feel their impact?

Our world is lost and has fallen into chaos, rebellion, and under the tyranny of the god of this world, the thief who came to kill and steal and destroy. We see the effects of that fallen, broken world every day—because it's our world. We see it on the news, we see it in our communities, in our places of work, and we've seen it in our family lives.

—from *Choosing to Learn from Life*, Chapter 3

31

Take a moment to remind your group that God created us all to live life with each other, to open ourselves up and become transparent with those we trust. Remember, learning *LifeShapes* is easier in the context of community. So take some time getting to know your group and helping them getting to know each other. Allow them to take some time together to answer the questions on page 32 of the participant workbook. Encourage participants to share significant moments that had an impact on their lives. Feel free to discuss only some questions as a group and encourage participants to explore the other questions on their own time.

REFLECT

Take a few minutes to answer these questions:

➤ What is a situation that happened recently in your own community that illustrates how malevolent the world has become?

➤ When you hear about events like the ones described in this reading, how do you respond internally? How do you respond externally?

➤ In what ways do you think God is present in those situations?

32

IF YOU ARE USING the DVD as part of your study, watch Chapter 3 now. Point out the fill-in-the-blank sections in the participant workbook and remind group members to watch for key words. After watching the segment, discuss these questions:

⮕ What ways do you see the kingdom of God at work around you right now?

⮕ How do you think your own life would be different if you went through the cycle of repent and believe on a regular or daily basis?

RESPOND　　　　　　　CHOOSING TO LEARN FROM LIFE WORKBOOK

AS YOU LEARN about the kingdom of God with your group, fill in the blanks in the sections below.

In the Gospels, we hear Jesus speak of the kingdom of God over and over, in his sermons, in his parables, and by his miracles. Jesus doesn't teach about a _____ kingdom that we can move to and swear allegiance to. The Greek word _____ means the kingdom or _____ of God.

It's coming and we'd better be ready! The story of the unexpected burglar in Matthew 24:42–44, the sudden arrival of the bridegroom in Matthew 25:1–13 and many other stories are pictures of the arrival of God's kingdom. It will come that quickly and change our lives that radically.

When we think of the kingdom of God, perhaps many of us think of heaven. And that certainly is a key aspect. Jesus spoke of the kingdom of God as being a future reality. Read Revelation 21:3–5.

⮕HUDDLES⮕　　*During the teaching time, Huddles extend the learning experience by encouraging interactions in small groups of 2 or 3.*

⮕HUDDLES⮕　　⮕ How does the description in these verses match up with your own picture of the kingdom of God?
_____
_____

Jesus doesn't leave the kingdom of God in the future. He makes it clear that he brings the kingdom of God. Now. In this life. He casts out demons, he heals miraculously, he disarms Satan. The kingdom is here! In Jesus,

33

---

*You can supplement the DVD segment with the following material, or use this material independently. Be sure to allow time to discuss the questions in the participant guide and Going Deeper questions as appropriate. You can find a fuller discussion of the kingdom of God in Chapter 4 of **Choosing to Learn From Life**.*

→ HUDDLES ←

Whenever you see the "Huddles" icon, have your group break up into Huddles of 2 or 3. Read the following paragraphs aloud, then give the Huddles a few minutes to discuss each question. Your group may stay in their Huddles while you present material from each section.

Slide 14

(Prepare Slides 14-30). Display Slide 14. **In the Gospels, we hear Jesus speaking of the kingdom of God over and over, in his sermons, in his parables and by his miracles.** *Display Slide 15.* **Jesus doesn't teach about a <u>geographic</u> kingdom that we can move to and swear allegiance to. The Greek word _basileia_ means the kingdom or <u>rule</u> of God.** *Display Slide 16.* **The kingdom refers to God's effective and powerful presence and influence in our lives.**

It's coming and we'd better be ready! The story of the unexpected burglar in Matthew 24:42–44, the sudden arrival of the bridegroom in Matthew 25:1–13 and many other

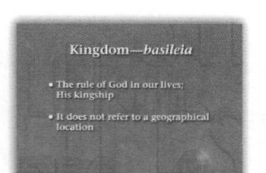

Slide 15

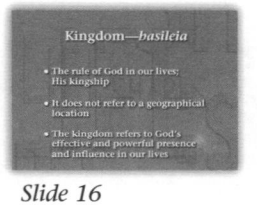

Slide 16

stories are pictures of the arrival of God's kingdom. It will come that quickly and change our lives that radically.

When we think of the kingdom of God, perhaps many of us think of heaven. And that's certainly a key aspect. Jesus spoke of the kingdom of God as being a future reality. Ask a volunteer to read Revelation 21:3–5.

→HUDDLES← ● How does the description in these verses match up with your own picture of the kingdom of God? (People will express various mental images.) ●

Jesus doesn't leave the kingdom of God in the future. He makes it clear that he brings with him the kingdom of God. Now. In this life. He casts out demons, he heals miraculously, he disarms Satan, he speaks with authority, he is master over the laws of nature. The kingdom is here! The power of the kingdom is undeniable. We know how the story will end—God will win the battle against evil—and we're drawn into the plot to experience the excitement from the inside.

Jesus was serious about the call to the kingdom of God. When we pray, "Your kingdom come," we are asking for God's rule to break into our lives, to influence the world, and bring us the reality of heaven.

GOING DEEPER:

● What do you think is the attitude of many Christians about the kingdom of God? *(Some might feel that most Christians are not expecting the kingdom of God; they don't look for it. Or it seems so far off that it doesn't feel real.)*

If the kingdom of God is near, how do we embrace it? Jesus says two things: repent and believe.

Display Slide 17. We often think of repentance as an outside thing. "I'm going to stop speeding." "I'm going to stop overeating." Actually, those behaviors may be the result of repentance, but repentance starts on the inside. The Greek word __metanoia__ means a <u>change of heart or mind</u>. *Display Slide 18.* It describes a process of transformation that takes place inside a person. In the process of repentance, we take a long, hard look at the *kairos* event. We ask questions about it, we talk to other people. We try to understand what happened and why we responded the way we did because we want to learn from the experience.

Display Slide 19. Believe is another action word. *Display Slide 20.* The Greek word __pisteuo__ means an active trust, taking action based on certainty you have in your heart. We show our faith in our actions. *Display Slide 21.* It can also be translated as faith. *Display Slide 22.* This is where we begin to change our actions. The inner changes that we have

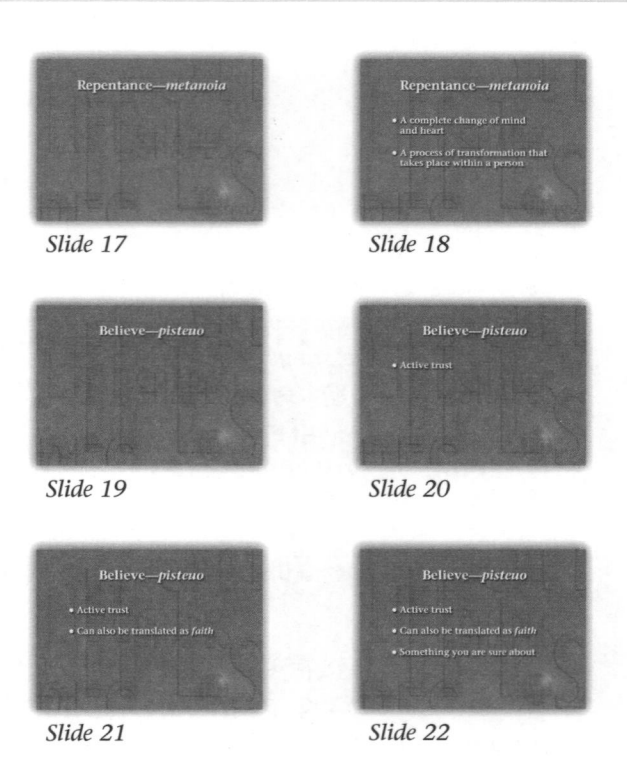

Slide 17

Slide 18

Slide 19

Slide 20

Slide 21

Slide 22

experienced in the process of repentance now start to impact our lives—the things we do and say.

We tend to think of repentance as an outward action and faith as an internal thing. Actually it is the other way around. Faith by its own definition is active; believing something and putting that belief into practice are inseparable.

→HUDDLES← ➡ Why is it important to put faith into action? *(The Bible says faith without action is no faith at all, James 2:26. Putting faith in action is one way of demonstrating the kingdom to others who may be ready to believe. It also draws us closer to God.)* ➡

GOING DEEPER:

➡ What are some ways that you put your faith into action? What makes it difficult to put belief into action?

Display Slide 23. **Time.** *Display Slide 24.* **Kingdom.** *Display Slide 25.* **Repentance.** *Display Slide 26.* **Faith.** These words are the heart of what it means to be a disciple. As if to underline the importance of discipleship, Jesus made a statement about discipleship as his last words before he went back to heaven. *Display Slide 27.* Ask a volunteer to read Matthew 28:18–20.

Slide 23

Slide 24

Display Slide 28. The word "disciple" in itself is important for us to understand. In Greek it's the word *mathetes*. The word means "<u>learner</u>" or "pupil." In some countries, such as Germany and Scandinavia, the native language translates the word *mathetes* with a popular word that they use for school students or students in a college or university. *Display Slide 29.*

But in English, we've used "disciple," a word that hardly anyone uses today outside of a religious setting. Actually it's not a religious word at all; it's simply a word that refers to somebody who chooses to learn. *Display Slide 30.*

Take a minute to think about your own personality. Are you open to new ideas? Are you excited to learn new things and discover ways that you can improve the way you live life? Change may be more difficult for some than others. Use this time of learning to explore how receptive you are toward becoming a lifelong learner.

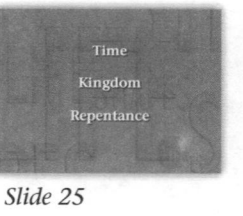

Slide 25

Slide 26

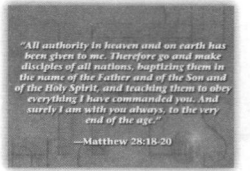

Slide 27

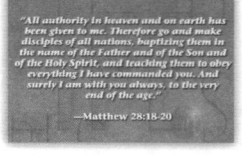

Slide 28

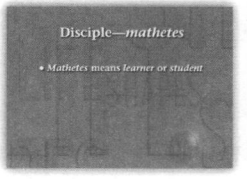

Slide 29

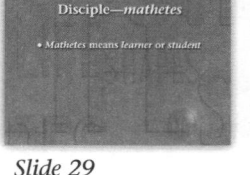

Slide 30

→HUDDLES←

◗ What prompts you personally to choose to learn something new in any area of your life? Do you have a different motivation in your spiritual life? *(Necessity sometimes motivates us to learn something new. We should see spiritual growth as a necessity. Disciples are learners. We also learn things that we get excited about, and God wants us to be excited about our relationship with him.)* ◗

GOING DEEPER:

◗ What is a difficult spiritual lesson that you have learned in the past? What spiritual lessons are you learning right now?

Jesus said this: Go out into all the world and make learners out of the people that you meet. If you've become a learner, then make other people learners. If you've learned how to lead from me, then go and teach other people how to learn from me. Go and disciple them, make them learners.

When we look at the Learning Circle, learn to understand these words, and apply them to our lives, we are learning what it means to be a disciple. A disciple is a learner.

→HUDDLES←

◗ How does understanding that a disciple is a learner change your ideas of discipleship? *(It makes it seem easier to understand. It becomes a relationship with Jesus instead of something that we're supposed to accomplish on our own. It's an ongoing process, not a destination.)* ◗

GOING DEEPER:

◗ Share a fundamental faith lesson that you've learned from someone in your life that has set Jesus' example.

ASK SOMEONE TO read aloud "*Kairos*: Learn and Change" from the participant's workbook, pages 36-37. Or, allow some quiet time for group members to read silently. Then discuss these questions as a group:

→ Have you ever had a period of time in your life when you bounced from crisis to crisis without any real change? What was that like for you?

→ Jesus says in order for us to experience true and lasting change, we need to repent and believe. What things do we do to short circuit or bypass the process of change? *(We often engage only one side of the Circle and ignore the steps of the other side. We ignore our own need for change and attempt to get others to change. We go no further in the process of change than compiling a list of advice.)*

KAIROS: LEARN AND CHANGE

WHAT ABOUT YOUR personal *kairos* event? What would it look like if the king were near? Your promotion at work, that new business deal—these present many opportunities for God's rule and influence to come into your life in a new way, affecting you family, your work colleagues, deepening your relationship with God. At that crisis point in your marriage, the king is near, bringing the wholeness that we look forward to in heaven into your daily situation. Your marriage and your family relationships could be revolutionized.

Whatever your *kairos* event, the king is near, to speak, to heal, to set free, to forgive, to restore, to influence—to rule as king! We need to learn from Jesus how to embrace it, how to get hold of it, to put our arms around everything that God wants to give us.

Jesus says we need to do two things to make the most of the opportunity: repent and believe the good news! We can only learn from our *kairos* events and experience God's rule through a process of repentance and belief. Without that process, we go from event to

event, crisis to crisis, repeating our mistakes, never seeing a lasting change. The Learning Circle describes the journey we make as we give God control of our *kairos* events and let him lead the way—the journey of repentance and belief. It is in this journey that we make our way closer and closer to the kingdom of God, becoming more like him, and drawing closer to him, with each passing challenge. It is on this journey that we can truly experience the intimacy with God and the power of his presence.

36

As you wrap up your session, point out the "Personal Challenge" on page 37 of the participant workbook. Allow some quiet time for individuals to write personal answers. Ask members to share the personal challenges that they have set for themselves with at least one other person. Encourage participants to prepare for the next session by answering the "Thinking Ahead" questions at the beginning of Session 4.

Discuss how to support each other's plans for personal challenges. Close your session with prayer.

As you begin to learn about what it means to be a true disciple of Jesus you are going to be faced with a difficult challenge: use this information to simply increase your knowledge *or* use this information to live a different life. When we learn new methods of discipleship or spiritual discipline, we tend to increase our knowledge base of God and his word, but we struggle with the actual implementation and change. *LifeShapes* makes this process easier but you still have to make the choice to put forth the effort. Take this to heart as you start to dig into the deeper areas of your life when answering these questions and sharing with your group. Be ready to share in the next session about your experiences with *kairos* and the kingdom of God this week.

PERSONAL CHALLENGE

➡ What *kairos* event are you facing right now from which you want to learn?

_____

_____

➡ To understand your *kairos* moment more fully, did God reveal any areas of your life that might need changed?

_____

_____

➡ To learn from your *kairos*, what faith action do you need to take this week?

_____

_____

37

_____
_____
_____
_____
_____
_____
_____
_____
_____
_____
_____
_____
_____
_____
_____
_____

4 THE LEARNING CIRCLE

IN THIS SESSION, YOUR GROUP WILL:

Learn how to respond
to *kairos* moments

•

Explore the concept
of repentance and what it
means to experience change

•

Discover how to put faith
into action in the context
of community

•

Form a plan to apply the Circle
to an individual *kairos* moment

Learning is a choice. When we make the choice to learn from Jesus, as he invites us to, we move deeper into the kingdom of God. In that realm we recognize the *kairos* moments where God is at work. Now the choice we face is how to respond to them. Choosing to enter the Learning Circle will deepen our walk of discipleship. Choosing to ignore or run away from the opportunity will do nothing but force us to remain superficial in our walk with God. *Kairos* moments become learning opportunities if we are willing to enter the process of repentance and belief.

PREPARATION:

- Read Chapters 4 and 5 from *Choosing to Learn from Life*.
- Read Jeremiah 29:11.
- If you are using the *Choosing to Learn from Life Teaching DVD,* or the *Learning Circle Slideshow* presentation, set up your equipment.
- Make sure you have a Bible to use in your session.
- Answer the discussion questions yourself so that you will have material for examples or prompting.

SCRIPTURAL BASIS:

- **Jeremiah 29:11** — This passage is often a source of encouragement and strength for many seeking God's guidance in their lives. Indeed, God desires good to come to all who seek him, but we sometimes forget that his blessings often come from times of challenge, the testing of our character, and our diligence in seeking to become more like Christ. God continually allows significant moments to occur in our lives in order to help us learn and change into the kingdom-minded disciples that he wants us to become.

KEY WORDS:

Repent
•
Observe
•
Reflect
•
Discuss
•
Believe
•
Plan
•
Account
•
Act

WELCOME YOUR GROUP members. As they come in, encourage them to review pages 39-40 of Session 4 and answer the "Thinking Ahead" questions. Now that they have learned to recognize *kairos* moments, invite participants to share some of their *kairos* moments during the past week and how they experienced the kingdom of God in those moments. Pray for continued understanding of the Circle. Ask group members to share and pray in small groups.

Then ask a volunteer to read aloud "No Going Back" from the participant workbook (page 41).

The questions on page 42 of the participant workbook are designed to get group members talking with one another. Don't force your group members to participate but encourage them to share their thoughts and feelings with others in the group. As participants grow closer to one another, they will begin to open up and

---

REFLECT

CHOOSING TO LEARN FROM LIFE WORKBOOK

NO GOING BACK

YOU'RE WALKING ALONG on what you think is a straight path; no unexpected bends in the road, no intersections where you have to make a decision you're not prepared for. Just a nice pleasant stroll. Suddenly out of nowhere an unplanned situation forces you to a screeching halt. You're at an intersection now, and you have to decide what to do, which way to go. It's a *kairos* moment.

You can pretend the moment never happened and hope its consequences will go away. You can dig in your heels and refuse to move in any direction at all. You can look behind you and move back to a familiar part of the path where you know what will happen.

Or you can pass through the portal and enter the Learning Circle. When a *kairos* moment occurs, we must decide whether to enter the Circle. From the moment we step into the Circle, we are in a learning mode. Things will not go back to the way they were before the *kairos* event.

If we don't step into the Circle, we don't learn from our *kairos* events. It can be hard work to stop doing things our way and let God have total control of our lives. But when we do, we give God the space to change us and lead us in a new direction.

—from ***Choosing to Learn from Life***, Chapter 4

41

---

become more transparent in their discussion. Be patient and respond positively when they share openly and honestly with the group. If necessary, allow your participants to spend more time getting to know each other and be intentional about getting to know them as well. This may take away from your teaching time but it will be invaluable in opening the doors to honest discussion.

If your group is small, you can do this all together. If you have a larger group, ask them to share in groups of 2 or 3. Covering all the questions is not as important as the quality and depth of the discussion.

REFLECT

Take a few minutes to answer the following questions:

⊙ Think about a *kairos* event in your life that revealed an area needing change. Discuss that situation and how it affected your life.

⊙ Discuss a *kairos* event in your life that you chose to disregard either by running away or simply ignoring God's prompting to change. How did that choice impact the "big picture" of that situation?

⊙ When something big happens in your life, good or bad, who or what do you immediately turn to for guidance or advice?

42

IF YOU ARE using the DVD as part of your study, watch Chapter 4 now. Point out the fill-in-the-blank sections around the blank Circle in the participant workbook and remind group members to watch for key words. After watching the segment, discuss these questions:

➔ Which of the Repent steps do you have the most difficulty with?

➔ Which of the Believe steps do you most need to work on?

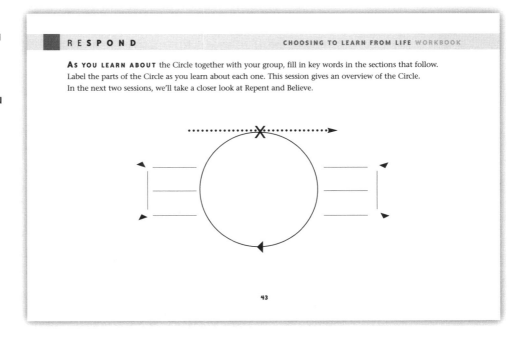

RESPOND   CHOOSING TO LEARN FROM LIFE WORKBOOK

AS YOU LEARN ABOUT the Circle together with your group, fill in key words in the sections that follow. Label the parts of the Circle as you learn about each one. This session gives an overview of the Circle. In the next two sessions, we'll take a closer look at Repent and Believe.

43

You can supplement the DVD segment with the following material, or use this material independently to explain the concepts of the Learning Circle. Be sure to allow time for Huddles in order to discuss the questions in the participant workbook and Going Deeper questions as appropriate for group discussion time. You can find a fuller discussion of the Learning Circle beginning with Chapter 4 of **Choosing to Learn from Life.**

→HUDDLES←

Whenever you see the "Huddles" icon, have your group break up into Huddles of 2 or 3. Read the following paragraphs aloud; then give the Huddles a few minutes to discuss each question. Your group may stay in their Huddles while you present material from each section.

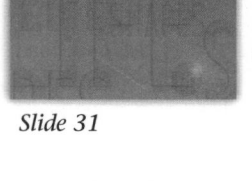

Slide 31

(Prepare Slides 31-42). Display Slide 31. **We do not become disciples of Jesus and stand still. Learning means we're constantly moving and growing. Jesus tells us to do two things to make the most of a** *kairos* **opportunity: repent and believe. We enter the Learning Circle.** *Display Slide 32.*

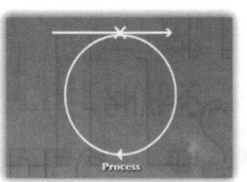

Slide 32

Display Slide 33. **The first half of the Circle is Repent.**

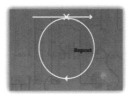

Slide 33

Display Slide 34. **The second half is Believe.**

Repentance is a process. We often equate the word "repent" with the confession of some sort of sin or bad behavior in our life, but the word itself actually means "to change one's mind." So, the process of repentance is not simply a response to sin, it is a response to our inner desire to do life differently. As we recognize our desire to make true and lasting change in our lives, we begin to do things that affect our outward actions. The steps in the first half of the Circle are the things we do that signify our willingness to recognize and process whatever it is about life that we want to be different.

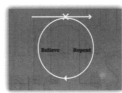

Slide 34

Display Slide 35. **To start the process of repentance, we observe our reactions, emotions, and thoughts. This has to be honest observation! It's not a time to defend ourselves or blame our actions on somebody else. It is about taking a *kairos* moment and simply exploring all of the inward spiritual, emotional, or mental circumstances that led to the occurrence of that event.**

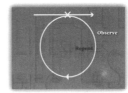

Slide 35

→HUDDLES← ➡ How much time do you spend on a daily basis intentionally exploring your own thoughts, feelings, or impressions about significant moments? ➡

Display Slide 36. **After observing, we reflect. Simple questions are a good start to the process of reflection. We want to ask ourselves questions that will help us discover the who, what, when, where, why, and how of the *kairos* moment and our response to it.**

Why am I feeling this way?

Why did I say that?

How did this happen?

→HUDDLES← ➡ Think of an event that triggered a strong emotional response in you. Discuss why you think you reacted the way you did. ➡

GOING DEEPER:

➡ What is your immediate reaction to discovering something new and interesting about yourself? How do you explore the emotional and spiritual side of that reaction?

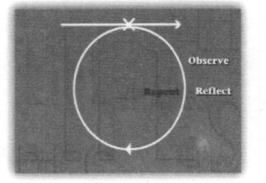

Slide 36

GOING DEEPER:

➡ As a group, formulate several *who, what, when, where, why,* and *how* questions that you could ask yourselves during this reflective stage.

Display Slide 37. **After observation and reflection, it's time for discussion. Now you invite others to look at the *kairos* event with you. Other people see things that we don't see for ourselves. They challenge us where we are reluctant to challenge ourselves. The best people to discuss with are people who will be completely honest, even if the things they say are not what we always want to hear. Discussion is a difficult phase for people because it involves openness and honesty.**

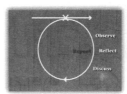

Slide 37

→**HUDDLES**← ◆ When you discuss *kairos* moments with someone, do you find yourself just giving the basic facts, or are you also sharing the deeper emotions and issues of your heart? ◆

Remind participants to add the labels of Observe, Reflect, and Discuss to the Circle diagram in their workbook. Make sure that the participants have a good understanding of the Repent side of the Circle before moving on to Believe. Discuss any questions that arise as a group.

GOING DEEPER:

◆ Why do we often tend to shy away from honest discussions? *(We don't want to appear weak; we're trying to justify our response; we're not sure that we want to be accountable for anything we say.)*

BELIEVE

Display Slide 38. Learning to move successfully through the Circle means that we must learn to go through both processes of repent and believe. If we only do one part, true change will not occur and God is certain to allow another *kairos* moment to happen so that we can experience the lasting change he desires for us. We learn by recognizing our desire to change and reflecting on that desire, but that is only the first step. Believing, or faith, means taking action. Faith, by its own definition, is active; believing in something and putting that belief into action are inseparable.

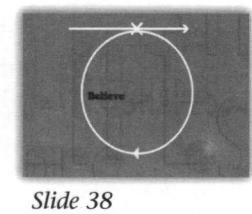

Slide 38

The Believe side of the Circle includes three parts:

<u>Plan</u>

<u>Account</u>

<u>Act</u>

Our faith does not rest in the hope of things that God promises us or tells us, it rests in God himself. We have an active trust in God that affirms his presence in our lives and assures us that he wants nothing but the best for us.

Display Slide 39. Faith is not simply sitting around and believing that God is going to make us change. Our faith is active and so the first step in our faithful response to a *kairos* moment is to plan. Planning is about vision, it is about having an intention to do something. As you take the information gained from

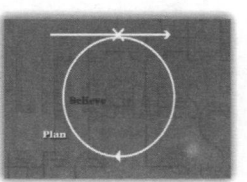

Slide 39

your observations, reflections, and discussions about a *kairos* moment, you can begin to create a plan that will affect your outward behavior. You have a vision of the end result, and you make a plan on how to get there. Making a plan is usually easy, implementing the plan is where people usually get hung up.

→HUDDLES← ➡ Taking your own personality into account, what kinds of things would help you to form and implement a plan? ➡

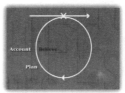

GOING DEEPER:

➡ As a group, formulate some clear characteristics of a good plan.

Display Slide 40. Then, if a plan is to be effective, we need at least one person to hold us accountable to it. Lasting change doesn't happen in private. It's pretty easy to cheat on a diet if no one else knows you're supposed to be on one. It doesn't take much to spend the down payment money on a weekend away if no one knows you were saving for a home.

We all know how easy it is to point out someone else's weak points. Jesus wants us to look inwardly at our own weaknesses and to allow another person to look alongside us.

Slide 40

→HUDDLES← ➡ Since plans are often easy to create but difficult to implement, do you think someone holding you accountable to your plan would help you with that process? ➡

Display Slide 41. **Now that you have a clear plan and someone to hold you accountable to that plan, it's time to take action. Faith bubbles up within us and rises to the surface where it turns into action. Faith is always acted out, never bottled up. Take your plan off the paper and into your life.**

Display Slide 42. Remind participants to fill in the labels of Plan, Account, and Act on the Believe side of the Circle diagram in their workbook.

In times of change, it's easy to pick through God's words and promises seeking sources of strength and encouragement (Jer. 29:11). As we do, we often get so caught up in the process of using scripture to make ourselves feel better that we forget it is God himself we should be trusting in. When you engage with scripture, do it in such a way that it deepens your understanding of and relationship with God. Life is full of trials and challenges, and it must be our trust in God that reassures us that those *kairos* moments, good and bad, are meant for our growth and maturity as his followers.

GOING DEEPER:

➡ Have you ever been in an accountability relationship? What was the best part and what was the most difficult part?

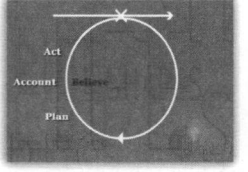

Slide 41

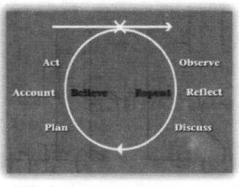

Slide 42

→HUDDLES← ➲ Discuss some clear moments in your life where it was both easy and difficult to take action on a plan.

This part of the Learning Circle is often the most difficult to implement because it's usually easier to recognize what needs changed in our lives but harder to implement true and lasting change. It's for this very reason that God regularly introduces new *kairos* moments that reveal to us the same pattern of behavior we are reluctant to change: that argument with our spouse over the same thing; the problem with our boss that keeps coming up. You get the picture. Making the process of change work for you depends on forming a good plan and allowing someone to hold you accountable to that plan. You must not skip from Discuss to Act (like we often do), rather, take advantage of each step in the Circle.

In learning to apply the Circle, you'll find that with your response to each *kairos*, the process of repentance and belief will lead to more of God's kingdom becoming present in your life. Each time around the Circle means that you have grown a little more and taken on a little more of the character of Christ.

GOING DEEPER:

➲ Why do we sometimes bail out instead of carrying through on a plan? *(We don't want our weakness exposed; we don't know how other people will respond—perhaps with rejection; it might not make any difference in the situation anyway.)*

ASK SOMEONE TO read aloud "Slinky Faith" from the participant's workbook, page 49-50. Or, allow some quiet time for group members to read silently. Then discuss these questions:

➔ Over the past couple of weeks, have you become more aware of *kairos* moments occurring in your life? How have you responded to those moments?

➔ The Learning Circle will often help change certain ways we outwardly behave. In what ways do you think the Circle will also change your spiritual and emotional behavior?

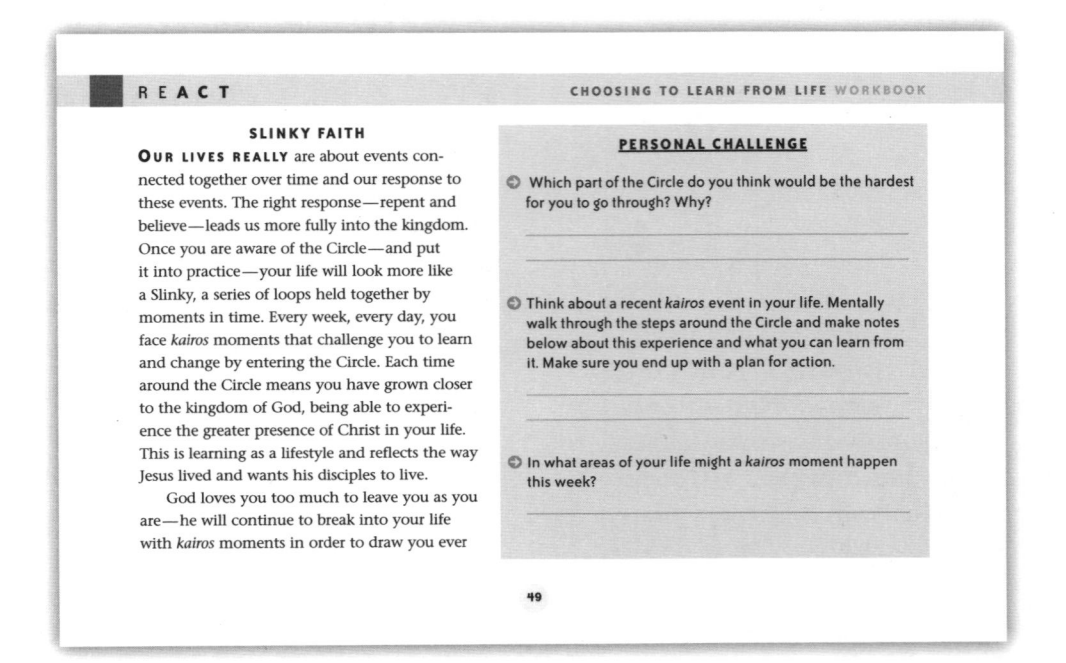

As you wrap up your session, point out the "Personal Challenge" on page 49 of the participant workbook. Allow some quiet time for individuals to write personal answers. Ask members to share the personal challenges that they have set for themselves with at least one other person in the group. Encourage participants to prepare for the next session by answering the "Thinking Ahead" questions at the beginning of Session 5.

Discuss how to support each other's plan for implementing these changes. Close your session with prayer.

closer to himself. To paraphrase Jesus in Mark 1:15, "I want you to enter into a lifestyle of repentance and faith; a lifestyle that is committed to learning from me what you need to know to be an effective representative of the kingdom. Listen to me and stay close to me, particularly in the moments I give you as opportunities to learn. Surrender to me— allow me to change you inwardly so that your attitudes and actions are constantly being renewed."

As you go through your life's journey this week, use the Circle diagram on the right side of this page to help you remember the steps you can take as you seek to grow and change in Christ. Be ready to share in the next session about your response to a *kairos* moment this week.

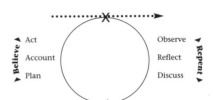

50

5 CHOOSING REPENTANCE

We teach our kids to say, "I'm sorry" before they can master pronouncing the "r" sound. If you have to repent, you must have done something wrong, right? Actually, no. The root of repentance is not judgment or deciding who was right and who was wrong. It's about deciding to change, deciding to turn in a new direction, deciding to learn from an experience. In the process of learning to follow Jesus more closely, we can have an infinite number of fresh starts each time we repent!

PREPARATION:

- Read Chapters 6, 7, and 8 from *Choosing to Learn from Life*.
- Read Numbers 13, 1 Samuel 17, and Acts 9.
- Make sure you have Bibles to use in your session.
- Answer the discussion questions yourself so that you will have material for examples or prompting.

SCRIPTURAL BASIS:

- **Numbers 13:2, 30** — Wanting the Israelites to act in faith—believing in his promise—God gives them a simple command: Observe. And from their observation, Caleb and Joshua are prompted to act on their faith and obey the Word of God.
- **1 Samuel 17:45** — Through his observation and reflections on his faith in God, David knows with confidence that his Lord is far greater than any weapon Goliath could possibly wield.
- **Acts 9:4-5** — Here is further evidence how much God wants to have a relationship with him that goes beyond dumping our petitions at his feet. He invites us to discuss life openly and honestly with him, even if he has to use extraordinary methods to open the dialogue, as he did with Paul.

KEY WORDS:

Repent
•
Observe
•
Reflect
•
Discuss

WELCOME YOUR GROUP members and encourage them to review pages 51-52 of Session 5 in the workbook including the "Thinking Ahead" questions. This lesson is the halfway point in your time together so it is a good idea to take the time to get some class feedback. Figure out what participants feel are positive portions of the class and what they might want to do differently. Make the appropriate changes as necessary so that everyone has the best experience with this material as possible.

Begin with a brief review of the Circle of Repent and Believe. Ask participants to share some of their experiences with repentance during the past week. Pray for continued understanding of the Repent side of the Circle.

Then ask a volunteer to read aloud "Nehemiah's Dilemma" from the participant workbook (page 53).

NEHEMIAH'S DILEMMA

NEHEMIAH WAS THE cupbearer to King Artaxerxes I. This position meant that he was one of the king's most trusted advisors. One day, Hanani, a fellow Jew, visited Nehemiah and told him about the state of Jerusalem. The city was in ruins, socially, physically, and spiritually. The news about Jerusalem broke Nehemiah's heart. Even though he had never been there, this was still his homeland, the land of his heritage. Nehemiah wept, fasted, and prayed for days asking God do something.

The king knew his cupbearer well. Nehemiah was in such distress that he couldn't hide it. When the king noticed a troubled expression on Nehemiah's face and asked what was wrong, Nehemiah took a chance and told the king about Jerusalem. God's hand was at work. Not only did the king give Nehemiah permission to go to Jerusalem, but he also gave him the resources to rebuild the city walls, the temple gate, and a house for himself! Nehemiah was on his way.

Nehemiah arrived in Jerusalem and stayed for three days, watching and waiting. He went out secretly at night to look at the city more closely. He spent time observing and reflecting upon the needs of the city.

Soon it was time to share his reflections with the city officials. The officials were inspired. "That sounds good. Let's start rebuilding." And they got right to work. After just a short time, the workers grew tired. Standing in rubble up to their necks made it seem like rebuilding a wall was impossible. And they were intimidated by frequent threats of the opposition.

Nehemiah understood that if Jerusalem was ever going to be rebuilt, it would take more than encouraging words. He needed a practical plan.

—from *Choosing to Learn from Life,*
Chapter 9

53

IF YOU ARE following these lesson plans rigidly, try breaking things up with a little bit of creativity and spontaneity. Perhaps you need to find new ways of involving people that have remained a little on the quiet side or involve the ones who have been very active in some of the teaching/leadership aspects of the class.

Every group is different. As the leader, you will need to figure out what works best for your group. You can trust the Holy Spirit to help you as you pray for your group and how best to lead.

Take a few minutes to answer these questions:

⊙ We are all leaders to some extent. As a leader, what is the most effective way to present a vision to those you lead?

⊙ How do emotions affect the repentance process?

⊙ Based on what you know about the Circle so far, what should be Nehemiah's first step?

54

Use this material to explain the concepts of the Repent side of the Circle. Be sure to allow time to discuss the questions in the participant guide and Going Deeper questions as appropriate. Point out the fill-in-the-blank sections in the participant workbook and remind group members to be listening for key words. You can find a fuller discussion of the Repent side of the Circle in Chapters 6–8 of Choosing to Learn from Life.

In Mark 1:14, Jesus' first command to us, the first part of the Circle, is to Repent. Sometimes this word makes us uncomfortable. We think of images of heavy-handed preachers handing out condemnation rather than grace. Repentance is not about judgment. It's about change.

As followers of Jesus, we are called continually to <u>change</u> how we think. Walking as a disciple of Jesus means constantly growing and changing inwardly as we take on more of the character of the Teacher. Every day—multiple times—we have the opportunity to say, "I'm not going to be like that any more. I'm not going to snap back at the sales person who can't answer my questions. I'm not going to yell at my kids about picking up their rooms. I'm not going to skip out of work early all the time." Repentance is not about judgment. It's about change.

Repentance is essential if we are to grow as <u>disciples</u> of Jesus, but most of the time it is not easy. Facing our failings is something we want to put off. But hiding or ignoring our failings does not make them go away. We have to see things as they really are if we are to change inwardly. This is not the time to look at how others have harmed us or insist that whatever happened is someone else's fault. It's not the time to say that what we've done is not as bad as what so-and-so did. It's time to be honest and open. Once we change on the inside, the new attitude will affect our outward behaviors.

→HUDDLES←

Whenever you see the "Huddles" icon, have your group break up into Huddles of 2 or 3. Read the following paragraphs aloud; then give the Huddles a few minutes to discuss each question. Your group may stay in their Huddles while you present material from each section.

OBSERVE

In Numbers 13 we read a story about how the Israelites got themselves into some serious trouble. Moses sent twelve spies to the land that God had promised to give the Israelites. Their mission? To observe. Look carefully and come back and tell everyone what they saw. Ask a volunteer to read Numbers 13:2 and 17–18.

Moses' instructions were specific. The observation had a purpose. Israel could use this information to decide where to settle or to plan battle strategies in order to take the land. Unfortunately, what they saw frightened off most of the people. Ten spies were looking at the wrong things. They didn't see God's promise fulfilled. They were frightened by what they saw.

"They will eat us alive."

"The people there are huge, like giants."

"We felt like grasshoppers next to them."

Fear spread to the rest of the people. Only <u>Caleb</u> and <u>Joshua</u> really saw what God intended them to see—the fulfillment of the promise he had made to his people. So instead of going into the new land, the Israelites spent the next forty years wandering in the desert.

It's easy to look at a situation and not see what is really there. Even when we start observation with the purpose of repentance and learning from the experience, we might see some scary stuff. It's not easy to be honest when we're looking closely at our own attitudes and behaviors.

When children learn to cross the road by themselves, they learn to <u>stop</u>, <u>look</u>, and <u>listen</u>. Sometimes we miss out on observation because we do not stop when a *kairos* event happens and look carefully at the situation.

Observation is more than looking. It's a fact-finding mission that leads to great discoveries. It involves all our senses. We remember the smell of a place, the taste of a favorite meal, and what it was like to touch something.

→HUDDLES←

◑ What kinds of things keep you from stopping to look closely when a *kairos* moment happens to you? *(Avoiding the challenge of change; too busy to think; don't want to admit possibility of being wrong.)* ◑

GOING DEEPER:

◑ What circumstances would help you observe a *kairos* event honestly and thoroughly? *(Being in a non-threatening situation; observing along with someone; not being afraid of being judged because of what turns up; having more experience with the process.)*

David was a musician, a victorious warrior, and a king who ruled for forty years. He is most remembered for something that happened when he was still a teenager. When no one else in Israel would accept the challenge that the giant Goliath taunted them with, David did (1 Sam. 17). And he wasn't even a soldier! He was just there to deliver food to his brothers. But he took stock of the situation and started asking questions.

Not everyone was interested in David's questions. His own brother Eliab essentially told him to be quiet and go back to his sheep. But David didn't give up.

Ask a volunteer to read 1 Samuel 17:26.

David's question showed that he had a purpose in asking them. In the words of his question, he shows his understanding of what the real battle is.

At the end of his reflections, David knew the answer to his questions: the Philistines did not have God's protection; Israel did. Anyone else who had reflected the way David had would have come to the same conclusion. Ask a volunteer to read 1 Samuel 17:45-49. Taking Goliath out took only a sling and a stone.

A simple way to reflect is to ask underlinequestions. Reflection is a common model of teaching in both the Old and New Testaments. When we ask questions about what we observe, we get below the surface to a deeper meaning of the experience. You've had an argument with your spouse, but what makes it a *kairos* is that it's the argument that you always have. You never seem to resolve this one. What reflections can you make about how you spoke, how you argued, why you walked away, and why you feel the way you do?

→HUDDLES←

➲ Make a list of questions that you could ask yourself during a *kairos* experience. Make sure this list echoes your own personality and tendencies. *(Personalized questions should reflect individual characteristics such as being introvert or extrovert, family or work context, tendency to rush to judgments, or avoid decisions, etc.)* ➲

DISCUSS

In Acts 9, we find out that Saul really had a thing about the Christians. He hated them with a passion! He was on his way to Damascus, to stir up serious trouble for Christians, when he had an unexpected discussion. Jesus himself gave Saul a life-changing *kairos* moment when he asked, <u>Saul, Saul, why are you persecuting me?</u> (Acts 9:4). Saul's answer was another question. <u>Lord, who are you?</u> (Acts 9:5). Jesus then lets Saul know about some changes that he wants to see. Instead of persecuting Christians, Saul would join them, and become Paul, the missionary to the Gentiles. What Paul knew about following Jesus as a disciple, he learned in that conversation in the middle of the road.

GOING DEEPER:

➲ Can you think of some Bible passages where Jesus encouraged his disciples to reflect by asking questions? *(Look at the birds of the air, Matt. 6; Who do you say that I am? Mark 8; Who touched me? Luke 8; Where shall we buy bread for these people? John 6; Who is your neighbor? Luke 10.)*

Later, when the New Testament church saw Gentiles become followers of Jesus, there was confusion. Some believed the Gentile men needed to be circumcised in order to be saved. Others, such as Paul and Barnabas, disagreed; surely believing in Jesus was the main thing. In the end Paul and Barnabas traveled to Jerusalem to meet with the elders and apostles there. Different opinions were shared. As a result of discussion, James, the leader of the church in Jerusalem, concluded that circumcision of Gentiles was not necessary. This decision, which arose out of discussion, shaped the church's mission to Gentiles from then on.

We need to get into the habit of discussion. We need to hear thoughts and reflections other than our own, and this takes humility and transparency. The process of discussion should take place with someone that you trust. It should be with someone who you know will not criticize or judge you but who will also be honest with you. Seek out friendships with people who will listen carefully to your observations and reflections. If this person truly understands what you are wanting to discuss, they will offer clear statements of empathy as well as sound bits of advice once it is appropriate to do so. Finding the right person to engage in discussion with will make it much easier for you to be open and honest. When you do this, the path of repentance and life change becomes clearer.

→HUDDLES← ● Why do we consider honesty so risky? ●

GOING DEEPER:

● Discussions sometimes get off track. What can you do to make sure a discussion about a *kairos* stays on the subject?

ASK SOMEONE TO read aloud "No Space Between Us" from the participant's workbook, page 59. Or, allow some quiet time for group members to read silently. Then discuss the following questions as a group:

➡ How can other people help you be more comfortable with "no space between us"? How can you help others be more comfortable?

➡ Share an experience of community that helped you grow in your faith.

NO SPACE BETWEEN US

IT SEEMS AS THOUGH our modern culture has created compartments for every aspect of our lives. We have our work compartment and our family life compartment and our church compartment and so on. We've even compartmentalized those compartments. Within our families, we've got our marriage in one compartment and our children in another. We have become a very neat and tidy society that does everything we can to keep our compartments from overlapping. After all, it would be perfectly absurd to share the personal details of our family life with our co-workers or talk to our children about a difficult time we are having at work! To make matters worse, our culture praises the principles of self-motivation and independence. The most successful people in life seem to be the ones who did it all on their own.

Yet, we can take one quick look at Jesus and realize that his life was not lived out in this way. There were no compartments in his life, there was no isolation, and there was no presumption dictating that everything he was to accomplish was going to be done entirely on his own. Jesus lived life in community. He shared every part of his life with his Father, with his disciples, and with the world around him. He always had someone to talk to, someone to eat with, someone to cry with, and someone to teach. Nowhere in Scripture is there a place to indicate a moment where Jesus wasn't doing life with somebody.

We talk so much about the need for our own personal space and privacy in personal matters, but the truth is that God designed us as people who need other people. True, there is nothing wrong with time alone to reflect or be with the Father, but the time for thinking that we "need our space" has come to an end. God created us to live in community and in that context, there is no space between us.

59

As you wrap up your session, point out the "Personal Challenge" on page 60 of the participant workbook. Allow some quiet time for individuals to write personal answers. Your group has just learned about the power of experiencing the processes of Observe, Reflect, and Discuss. Give them some time at the end of this session to go through those processes regarding this material. At the end of their time together ask them to share the personal challenges that they have set for themselves with at least one other person in the group. Encourage participants to prepare

These ideas about compartmentalization and isolation are completely counter-cultural. They probably sound very different from the ideas of independence and self-reliance that many of us have been brought up to believe. You may or may not agree but you need not go any further than the Bible and the teachings of Jesus to see that this is contrary to the way in which our Master and Teacher lived his life. Community and transparency are at the core of *LifeShapes*. If you are going to be successful in implementing the principles of the Circle and if you are going to continue your study of the other *LifeShapes*, you will continue to face the challenges of community, transparency, and openess in your life. Be thinking in the coming weeks about this as you answer the questions and share with your peers. Be ready to share in the next session about your experiences with repentance this week.

PERSONAL CHALLENGE

⊝ This is a very challenging idea. Do you agree or disagree with the ideas of de-compartmentalizing your life?

⊝ Describe a situation in your life right now that calls for a drastic change in the way you isolate parts of your life.

⊝ Name someone about whom you can say, "No space between us."

60

for the next session by answering the "Thinking Ahead" questions at the beginning of Session 6.

Discuss how to support each other's plans for personal challenge. Close your session with prayer.

6 CHOOSING A NEW DIRECTION

IN THIS SESSION, YOUR GROUP WILL:

Learn the three phases of Believe

•

Explore biblical examples of the phases of Believe

•

Discover the power of community

•

Form a plan to enter the Repent side of the Learning Circle

Do you ever feel (even if secretly) a little extra pressure to be an example of belief and faith to those around you? Maybe you think you need to know all the theological answers or be able to recognize any verse from the Bible with just a one-word clue. Faith is not so much about what we know as what we do. We follow Jesus as his disciples. We want to be like him. We want to take the kind of action that he took to show God's power in people's lives. This session will remind everyone in your group that God wants us to put feet on our faith.

PREPARATION:

- Read Chapters 9, 10, and 11 from *Choosing to Learn from Life*.
- Read Matthew 6:33–34 and 7:24; 1 Samuel 20.
- Make sure you have Bibles to use in your session.
- Answer the discussion questions yourself so that you will have material for examples or prompting.

SCRIPTURAL BASIS:

- **Matthew 6:33-34** — Throughout Scripture, Jesus outlines the plans he has for the disciples—even giving them ways to form their own plans. Some plans were short and simple, like the one in this passage, while others were more complex. Regardless of their detail, all of Jesus' plans were designed to help the disciples, and us, act out in faith.

- **1 Samuel 20:14-15** — David and Jonathan shared a great friendship. The depths of their relationship gave them someone to turn to and ask for help in times of need. It is this kind of accountability that we should all strive for in our relationships.

- **Matthew 7:24** — With this one sentence, Jesus sums up the final stage in the process of Repentance and Belief: take action. Through our faithful actions, Jesus gives us the assurance that we will always have a solid rock to stand on and trust in during times of trouble.

KEY WORDS:

Believe

•

Plan

•

Account

•

Act

WELCOME YOUR GROUP members. As they come in, encourage them to review pages 61-62 of Session 6 and answer the "Thinking Ahead" questions.

Begin with a brief review of the Repent side of the Circle. Invite participants to share some of the experiences they reflected on the past week. Pray for continued understanding of the Repent side of the Circle. Depending on the size of your group, you may want to share experiences and pray together in small groups.

Then ask a volunteer to read aloud "Not According to Plan" in the participant workbook (page 63).

RE**FLECT**

CHOOSING TO LEARN FROM LIFE WORKBOOK

NOT ACCORDING TO PLAN

YOU WANT TO BE a better spouse, so you book a meal at an exclusive restaurant. You know you need to spend more time with the children, and your mind starts planning a weekend full of together time, just hanging out, doing things your kids like to do. You know you should set a stronger Christian example at work, so okay, you're going to get right on that and start witnessing.

So you tell your spouse about the delightful dinner surprise and in return get a reminder that you have an important parent-teacher conference your spouse has told you about every day for the past week. You tell your children that you want to hang out with them all weekend, and they groan. They are all scheduled for sleepovers at their friends' houses. They asked permission, and you said yes. Now it looks like you have changed your mind. Your enthusiasm comes across as pressure to do something they don't want to do. And your work colleagues? You invite someone to church, and the person expresses a hatred for organized religion and you have no idea what to say next.

That went well, didn't it?

You were trying to live a passionate life and all you managed to do was confuse your wife, annoy your children, and alienate your work colleagues! Great!

The first stage of faith is not, "Just do it!" It is to make a plan.

—from ***Choosing to Learn from Life,*** Chapter 9

63

The questions on page 64 of the participant workbook are designed to break the ice and begin conversation among the group. Ask the group to share answers to the discussion questions on page 64 of the participant workbook.

Encourage participants to share revealing moments that had an impact on the life of someone else. Feel free to discuss only some of the questions as a group and encourage participants to explore the other questions on their own time.

Hopefully your group is comfortable enough by now to share personal and honest answers with each other but remain sensitive to those, including any newcomers, who may not be.

Take a few minutes to answer these questions:

○ Give an example of how "real life" sometimes get in the way of great plans.
_____
_____

○ As the person in this story, what do you think you could have done differently?
_____
_____
_____

○ When your plans get spoiled, are you more likely to try again or just give up? Explain.
_____
_____
_____

64

Use this material to explain the concepts of the Believe side of the Circle. Encourage participants to be listening for key words to fill-in-the-blanks in the participant workbook. Be sure to allow time to discuss the questions in the participant guide and Going Deeper questions as appropriate. You can find a fuller discussion of the Believe side of the Circle in Chapters 9–11 of Choosing to Learn from Life.

→HUDDLES←

Whenever you see the "Huddles" icon, have your group break up into Huddles of 2 or 3. Read the following paragraphs aloud; then give the Huddles a few minutes to discuss each question. Your group may stay in their Huddles while you present material from each section.

In the last session, the last stage of Repentance was Discussion. This presents us with the chance to bring clarity and focus to the changes God wants to bring to our lives. But what happens next? You might be tempted to jump right into action. But the first stage of faith is not, "Let's just do it!" It is to make a plan.

PLAN

The people of Israel had been in exile in Babylon for several generations. A new king allowed some of them to return to Canaan. News came to Nehemiah, the king's Hebrew cupbearer, that Jerusalem was in shambles. Socially, physically, and spiritually, the city was a disaster. Nehemiah was devastated and wanted to help. With the king's permission and financial backing, he went to Jerusalem to rally the people and organize the work of rebuilding Jerusalem. Nehemiah had a plan, and that's what it took to get this job done.

Nehemiah understood that if Jerusalem was ever going to be rebuilt, it would take more than encouraging words and the permission of the city officials. He needed a practical <u>plan</u> that would empower the Israelite people and deal with their enemies. His plan must enable them to carry on with the practicalities of rebuilding the wall of Jerusalem as well as strengthen their identity as God's people.

So Nehemiah put his systems into place. He began with a close inspection of what needed to be done—just how bad the destruction was. Then he inspired the people with his experience with the king and the support the king offered. The Israelite people were pumped up. Officials of some of the other people in the area were not so excited. In fact, they were determined to sabotage everything Nehemiah did. But Nehemiah planned well. He placed guards at strategic places, made sure workers had weapons should they need them, and set up a work schedule that kept the project moving forward despite the opposition.

It wasn't an easy job, but Nehemiah stuck to the plan and got the job done. Perhaps we don't think of planning as an activity that is full of faith. But look at some of the great projects of the Bible. They could not have been accomplished without a plan: the Exodus under Moses, the conquest of the land under Joshua, building the temple under Solomon, or Paul's mission to the Gentiles. These projects were huge undertakings that showed God's kingdom power in action.

Ask a volunteer to read Matthew 6:33–34. **The key to any plan is God's <u>kingdom</u>. We seek that first, and God takes care of the rest.**

→HUDDLES← ⟳ In practical terms, what does it mean to seek first the kingdom of God? *(We must ask ourselves if we are looking for ways to bring glory to God and make his kingdom visible. We might have to reevaluate our priorities, how we spend our time and use our resources, with that goal in mind.)* ⟳

GOING DEEPER:

⟳ If you were truly able to let go of worrying about tomorrow, how would your life be different?

ACCOUNT

When King Saul threatened David's life repeatedly, Jonathan, Saul's son, helped David get away to safety. But before the friends parted, Jonathan asked for one thing: "Remember that we have a covenant of friendship, and if I die, keep that covenant with my family" (1 Sam. 20:14–15).

Jonathan did die in battle, as did his father. David became king and remembered the promise he had made. Although Jonathan was dead, David was accountable for what he had said he would do. He searched for a member of Jonathan's family and found his son Mephibosheth, who had been disabled as a child. David took Mephibosheth into his own household and treated him like a member of his own family.

How many of us have started a new year with intentions to spend more time with the children, lose weight, be nice to that difficult character at work, spend more time with God, or stop speeding—only to fail by the end of the first week? If a plan is going to be effective, then we need at least one person who is going to hold us accountable for it. Remember, faith is not a private thing, and change does not happen in private.

Accountability is not someone else telling you what to do. Accountability is asking another person to help you do the things you already want to do. These relationships help you stick to the <u>plans</u> you've made and take the steps you want to take. We are not forced to be <u>accountable</u>, but we ask friends to help us by holding us accountable.

Our best plans can easily be reduced to a pile of good intentions when we try to accomplish them under our own steam. An accountability friendship is a cross between a cheerleader and a coach. Your friend cheers you on, but like a coach, this person is not afraid to challenge you and push you harder.

Accountability was a way of life for the disciples. Notice that whenever Jesus sent the disciples out to accomplish a task, he always sent them out in pairs. At all times, they were accountable to each other for their tasks and their behavior. They continued this practice all throughout their ministries. We, too, need to develop the kind of friendship where we can invite trusted friends to hold us accountable.

→HUDDLES←

➋ What is it about the word "accountability" that makes us uncomfortable? *(It means being vulnerable; letting others see our failures; making a commitment that might mean sacrifice in another area of our lives. We don't like to be pinned down.)* ➋

GOING DEEPER:

➋ How do you think your life would change if you had the kind of accountability relationship described here?

ACT

The disciples spent three years with Jesus, learning from him and discovering what it meant to enter the kingdom of God. Eventually it would become clear whether they would act on those values of discipleship

Judas wanted to live his life by his priorities, not God's. He went to the religious leader and arranged to betray Jesus in exchange for money. After Jesus was arrested and Judas realized what he had done, he took his own life.

When Jesus went to the cross, the disciples scattered. Peter denied knowing him. Only John was present at the cross.

But after the resurrection, the disciples were ready to move forward. Before Jesus returned to his Father, he gave them a job to do, and they organized themselves to do it. On Pentecost they were filled with the Holy Spirit. For the rest of their lives, the disciples pointed people to Jesus. They lived as a community, sharing their possessions. They boldly preached the message of Jesus in spite of violent opposition and great personal cost.

At the end of the Sermon on the Mount, Jesus puts out a challenge. Ask a volunteer to read Matthew 7:24–27. The people who truly follow Jesus not only hear what he says but also do it. They take action.

→HUDDLES←

◗ Describe an experience when you were able to move all the way around the Circle by putting a plan into action. Have you experienced lasting change as a result of your actions? ◗

GOING DEEPER:

◗ Describe a time when you were unwilling or unmotivated to put a plan into action. What did you learn from that experience?

ASK SOMEONE TO read aloud "Decision Time" from the participant's workbook, page 69. Or, allow some quiet time for group members to read silently. Then discuss these questions:

➡ Do you make decisions quickly or think about things for a long time first? Explain.

➡ What one thing most motivates you to take action? *(Urgency of need; sense of conviction — or guilt; compassion; love; sense of injustice.)*

R E **A C T**

CHOOSING TO LEARN FROM LIFE WORKBOOK

DECISION TIME

YOU HAVE TO make a decision.

Action comes out of confidence. It's a faith issue.

Sometimes our lives are shaped by inactivity. We sit around thinking about what we should do, maybe even talk about how we should go about doing it. But somehow it never gets done. Underneath, we're not really sure if it's right. Or we're not sure we're up to the job, and if we procrastinate long enough, perhaps the opportunity will pass, and we won't really have to try. Or we tell ourselves we're not ready yet; we need to go back to earlier sections of the Circle. Maybe we reflect a little longer, talk a little longer, or make more plans. But there comes a point where our confidence is expressed in how we live. It is visible, it is seen, it is public. The changes are out there for everyone to see.

Jesus has always been much more than just talk. He preached and taught, but he also loved, healed, and lived among people. Every story we read about Jesus' life we see a moment where he stepped out in boldness and lived a life of action and decision. He knew that he only had a limited amount of time to impact the lives of the people he was with so he was constantly following up his teachings and observations with action. Because we're his disciples we want to live the way he lived—a life of active faith.

Be ready to share in the next session about your experiences with the Believe side of the Circle.

69

As you wrap up your session, point out the "Personal Challenge" on page 70 of the participant workbook. Allow some quiet time for individuals to write personal answers. Ask members to share the personal challenges that they have set for themselves with at least one other person in the group.

Encourage participants to prepare for the next session by answering the "Thinking Ahead" questions at the beginning of Session 7.

Discuss how to support each other's plans for personal challenge. Close your session with prayer.

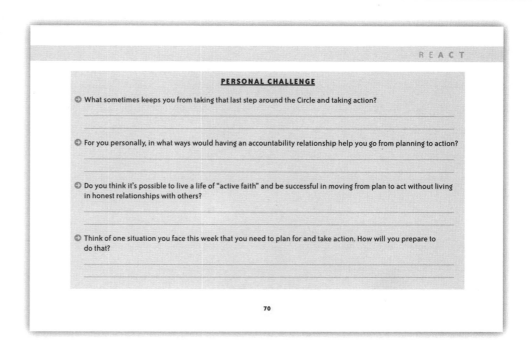

PERSONAL CHALLENGE

➲ What sometimes keeps you from taking that last step around the Circle and taking action?

➲ For you personally, in what ways would having an accountability relationship help you go from planning to action?

➲ Do you think it's possible to live a life of "active faith" and be successful in moving from plan to act without living in honest relationships with others?

➲ Think of one situation you face this week that you need to plan for and take action. How will you prepare to do that?

70

7 THE CIRCLE IN THE BIBLE

IN THIS SESSION, YOUR GROUP WILL:

Learn how Jesus used the Circle to teach his disciples

•

Explore how the disciples learned from the Circle

•

Discover how to apply the biblical example to their lives

•

Form a plan to apply the Circle to *kairos* moments in their lives

You and your group have spent the last several sessions learning how to apply and live out the processes of the Circle. We spend a great deal of time emphasizing that the central focus of *LifeShapes* is doing life exactly as Jesus did it. You have seen several scriptural examples that point to bits and pieces of the Circle but now it's time to focus on a single event in the life and ministry of Jesus where he took his followers through the entire Circle. Use this study of the Sermon on the Mount to explore the life of Jesus and make your own personal applications of this powerful tool.

PREPARATION:

- Read Matthew 5–7.
- If you are using the *Choosing to Learn from Life Teaching DVD* or *Learning Circle Slideshow* presentation, set up your equipment.
- Make sure you have Bibles to use in your session.
- Answer the discussion questions yourself so that you will have material for examples or prompting.

SCRIPTURAL BASIS:

- **Matthew 6:25-27** — In this passage, we can clearly see how Jesus used the principles of the Circle. In just a few short sentences, he highlights the steps of observation, reflection, and discussion in an effort to guide his disciples through the process of repentance and life-long change.
- **Matthew 7:1, 3** — As we live out our faith, Jesus calls upon us not to judge others with criticism or condemnation but to lift one another up in friendship and accountability. This is the level of authentic community God calls us to live.

KEY WORDS:

Repent
•
Observe
•
Reflect
•
Discuss
•
Believe
•
Plan
•
Account
•
Act

WELCOME YOUR GROUP members. As they come in, encourage them to review pages 71-72 of Session 7 and answer the "Thinking Ahead" questions.

Begin with a brief overview of the Circle. Now that your participants are more comfortable in class discussion and know all the elements of the Circle, spend these last few sessions talking and sharing about experiences where all the various phases of the Circle were involved. Pray for continued understanding of the Circle.

Then ask a volunteer to read aloud "Starting Point" from the participant workbook (page 73).

STARTING POINT

GO TO A CHRISTIAN bookstore and peruse the shelves that hold books about discipleship. Do you like what you see? Or are you overwhelmed by what you see? Where do you start? Bible study? Prayer? Practical theology? Small groups? Individual studies? Life topics? Book study? What's even worse is the fact that among the hundreds of books regarding the same subject matter, each one presents an entirely different idea about how to live life. Which one is the right one?

And then pick up a secular newspaper or magazine. Chances are you'll stumble across something about Christians, whether they are characterized as right wing fanatics with abortion protest signs or simply the growing bulge of middle America who claim to go to church two or more times each month.

When you decide that you want to deepen your spiritual experience, how do you even know where to begin?

The answer is simpler than you think: Look at Jesus. Learn from him. The first disciples walked the roads of Galilee and Judea with Jesus for three years. The gospels give us accounts of those experiences, so that we, too, can learn from Jesus. Every example we need to live any part of our lives as God would have us is clearly presented in the life of one man.

—from *A Passionate Life*,
Chapter 1

73

95

Use the questions on page 74 of the participant workbook to get conversation started among the group members. Ask the group to share answers to the discussion questions on page 74 of the participant workbook. Continue to encourage participants to share revealing moments that had an impact on other people's lives. Feel free to discuss only some of the questions as a group and encourage participants to explore the other questions on their own time.

Take a few minutes to answer these questions:

◑ When you want a deeper spiritual experience, what kind of things do you look for to help you?

_____

_____

◑ Think back to the last time that you read one of the gospels straight through in order to better understand the life of Jesus. What was that experience like for you?

_____

_____

◑ In just three or four words, how would you characterize the earthly ministry of Jesus?

_____

_____

74

IF YOU ARE using the DVD as part of your study, watch Chapter 5 now. Point out the fill-in-the-blank sections in the participant workbook and remind group members to be watching for key words and labels. After watching the segment, discuss these questions as a group:

◉ How does seeing the whole Circle in one passage of Scripture help you understand it better?

◉ Jesus wants us to put his words into practice. How do we do that?

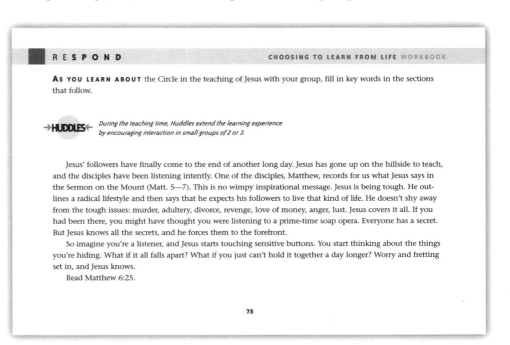

RESPOND   CHOOSING TO LEARN FROM LIFE WORKBOOK

AS YOU LEARN ABOUT the Circle in the teaching of Jesus with your group, fill in key words in the sections that follow.

→HUDDLES← *During the teaching time, Huddles extend the learning experience by encouraging interaction in small groups of 2 or 3.*

Jesus' followers have finally come to the end of another long day. Jesus has gone up on the hillside to teach, and the disciples have been listening intently. One of the disciples, Matthew, records for us what Jesus says in the Sermon on the Mount (Matt. 5—7). This is no wimpy inspirational message. Jesus is being tough. He outlines a radical lifestyle and then says that he expects his followers to live that kind of life. He doesn't shy away from the tough issues: murder, adultery, divorce, revenge, love of money, anger, lust. Jesus covers it all. If you had been there, you might have thought you were listening to a prime-time soap opera. Everyone has a secret. But Jesus knows all the secrets, and he forces them to the forefront.

So imagine you're a listener, and Jesus starts touching sensitive buttons. You start thinking about the things you're hiding. What if it all falls apart? What if you just can't hold it together a day longer? Worry and fretting set in, and Jesus knows.

Read Matthew 6:25.

75

You can supplement the DVD segment with the following material, or use this material independently. Be sure to allow time for Huddles in order to discuss the questions in the participant workbook and the Going Deeper questions as appropriate.

→**HUDDLES**←

Whenever you see the "Huddles" icon, have your group break up into Huddles of 2 or 3. Read the following paragraphs aloud; then give the Huddles a few minutes to discuss each question. Your group may stay in their Huddles while you present material from each section.

(Prepare Slides 43-54). **Jesus' followers have finally come to the end of another long day. Jesus has gone up on the hillside to teach, and the disciples had been listening intently. One of the disciples, Matthew, records for us what Jesus says in the Sermon on the Mount (Matt. 5—7). This is no wimpy inspirational message. Jesus is being tough. He outlines a radical lifestyle and then says that he expects his followers to live that kind of life. He doesn't shy away from the tough issues: murder, adultery, divorce, revenge, love of money, anger, lust. Jesus covers it all. If you had been there, you might have thought you were listening to a prime-time soap opera. Everyone has a secret.**

But Jesus knows all the secrets, and he forces them to the forefront. He's putting some pressure on his disciples to really understand what this kingdom business is all about. He has just been healing the sick and casting out demons and doing amazing things. Now he wants his disciples to understand what all that has to do with their lives.

Ask a volunteer to read Matthew 6:25.

 HUDDLES ➲ How would you respond if you were trying to hide your worry and somebody revealed it? ➲

> **GOING DEEPER:**
>
> ➲ What kinds of things do you do to hide your worry?
>
> ➲ Tell about a time when you were able to truly let go of worry.

Jesus knows what is happening in his listeners' hearts, so he takes them through a process that will set them free. The moment of worry is a *kairos* moment. Jesus sees on a daily basis what his disciples, and the average person listening to him preach, worry about. Things like food, clothes, finances, etc. Something happens in life to spark worry about any given issue and Jesus teaches that our response must be, rather than fruitless worry, to use our thoughts and feelings in directing us through a process of growth and change. By stepping into the Circle, the disciples—and we—can learn even from an experience of worry. We can see in the Sermon on the Mount how Jesus goes around the Circle of Repent and Believe. Jesus goes right through the six steps.

OBSERVE

Display Slide 43. Ask a volunteer to read Matthew 6:26. **In the Sermon on the Mount, the listeners are at a *kairos* moment. Jesus outlined a radical lifestyle in response to *kairos*. He begins with Repentance.** *Display Slide 44.*

Display Slide 45. **Jesus prods his followers to observe. "Look at the <u>birds of the air</u>." What do we notice when we look at the birds? We worry, but the birds don't. They don't store up food, but they have enough to eat. God feeds them, and he is going to feed us too. In fact, he's going to take care of everything we need. In observing the birds, the disciples end up looking at themselves and their own lack of faith.**

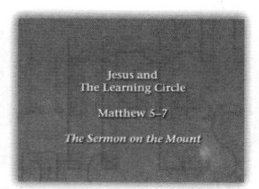

Slide 43

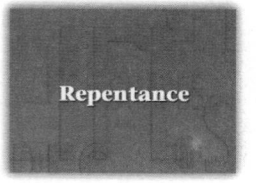

Slide 44

REFLECT

Display Slide 46. **So they look at the birds. Then Jesus says, "Are you not much more <u>valuable</u>?" Of course the answer is yes. Through reflection, Jesus helps his disciples put things in perspective. He makes them look at something outside of themselves so they can see something about themselves. "What about the flowers?" Jesus says. "What about the lilies?" The disciples may not know exactly where Jesus is going with all this, but they're listening. They're observing. They're reflecting.**

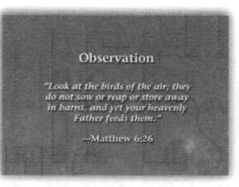

Slide 45

DISCUSS

Display Slide 47. Ask a volunteer to read Matthew 6:27. **Matthew doesn't give us a word-for-word record of the discussion between Jesus and the disciples. However, we do know that the usual teaching method in that day was question-and-answer. Jesus was a rabbinical teacher. That means he used question-and-answer as a standard teaching method. So he's not making rhetorical statements. He really is asking these questions, and there really is a right answer. Jesus invites the disciples to enter the discussion process together.**

Slide 46

Display Slide 48. Observation. Reflection. Discussion.

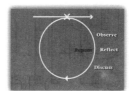

Slide 47   *Slide 48*

 →HUDDLES←

➜ What strikes you most about the Observe-Reflect-Discuss process recorded in this passage? *(Allow participants to respond freely. There are no right or wrong answers.)* ➜

GOING DEEPER:

➜ How can you apply your own observation about the Repent process to a situation in your life?

PLAN

Display Slide 49. **So how do we build a life that is not based on worry but on faith?** Ask a volunteer to read Matthew 6:33.

Display Slide 50. **This is the clearest statement on planning that the Bible gives us. Jesus wants us to make plans for his kingdom and righteousness. Righteousness means <u>right relationship</u>. When the rule of God comes into our lives, we let go of our worries. Jesus is saying that with the rule of God in our lives, he's in charge. We need to let him be in charge of our finances, our families, everything we do. We can choose to surrender to the king and follow his plan. Every plan that we formulate in response to a *kairos* moment should take into account our relationship with God. Planning is not simply working toward a solution to the problem or a specified goal of personal change. Great planning includes involving and inviting God into the process with us.**

As you formulate your plans and goals, discover the steps you can take to strengthen and deepen your relationship with him. How is God involved in your financial plan? How is he involved in your plan to strengthen relationships within your family? How is God present in the plans you form as a response to everything you worry about? Jesus wants to be a part of your plans and the plans that truly succeed are those that involve him!

Slide 49

Slide 50

ACCOUNT

Display Slide 51. **After the plan comes accountability.** Ask a volunteer to read Matthew 7:1–3. **Jesus keeps us humble! He reminds us of our own frail and inadequate self-protectiveness. He's not calling us to judge each other but to look at ourselves and remember that we are <u>accountable</u> for the choices and plans we make in a life of discipleship. Jesus wants us to look inward at ourselves, not asking how or what we can do to change other people for the better, rather what we can do to change ourselves for the better.**

Slide 51

Then right in the middle of the chapter, Jesus compares accountability to fruit. Ask a volunteer to read Matthew 7:18. *Display Slide 52.* **Good trees don't bear bad fruit. Bad trees don't bear good fruit. Which kind of tree are you going to be? What kind of person are you? Remeber something important: There are people all around you who will experience the consequences of the choices you make. Will you make good choices or will you make poor choices? Jesus wants you to find somebody to hold you accountable for the choices you make. Does your life reveal the kingdom of God where you live?**

Slide 52

When you squeeze a lemon, you get lemon juice. When you squeeze a Christian, what should come out? Christ. *Kairos* **moments squeeze us. What does the world see coming out of us?**

ACT

Let's go back to the story of the wise and foolish builders that we touched on in the last session. Jesus tells the crowd about two men. One builds a house on rock, the other on sand.

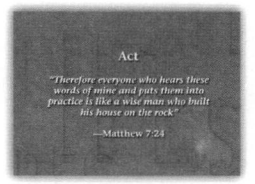

Display Slide 53. Ask a volunteer to read Matthew 7:24–27. **When we remember everything that came before this story in the Sermon on the Mount, starting with the Beatitudes right through to warnings about false prophets, we see what Jesus is getting at. Everybody was listening that day. The foolish builder and the wise builder were both listening. The ones who listen and then go out and put faith into action are the true followers of Jesus. The wise man who built his house on the rock listened to what Jesus said and then did what Jesus said to do.**

Your observations, reflections, discussions, plans, and even your accountability to someone else is completely useless if you do not act on what you have learned and your plans for change. *Kairos* **moments are events that often reveal areas of your life that God would like you to improve upon for his glory. People often get frustrated or even angry with God when they feel like the same bad thing keeps happening to them over and over. The truth is that people often fail to act on their plans and as a result, God has to keep moving them through the Circle until they finally get what it is that he wants them to understand and change. The wise followers of Christ are the ones who carry through with their plans; moving closer to the kingdom and growing in their intimacy with Jesus in the process.**

Slide 53

Display Slide 54. **Jesus has brought the disciples around the Learning Circle. "The time has come; the kingdom of God is near. Repent and believe the good news!" (Mark 1:15.)**

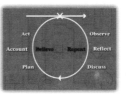

Slide 54

So simple to understand but often, so difficult to do. Our lives on earth will never be perfect, nor will we ever be able to experience all the change that God desires from us using the Circle, but that is exactly why he has given us grace. He is always proud of our growth as Christians and he is always forgiving of our failures as fallen humans. Practicing the Circle, starting with the smaller *kairos* events of your life, is the key to learning how deep you can truly go in your relationship with Jesus. Likewise, teaching the Circle to others and enabling them to experience the power of Repent and Believe, will aid in your understanding of the Circle and your ability to use it in the most difficult of circumstances.

→HUDDLES← ➜ What strikes you most about the Plan-Account-Act process described in this passage? ➜

GOING DEEPER:

➜ How can you apply your own observation about the Believe process to a situation in your life?

ASK SOMEONE TO read aloud "One Step Further" from the participant's workbook, page 79. Or, allow some quiet time for group members to read silently. Then discuss these questions as a group:

⊙ What was so radically different about the ideas that Jesus taught? *(He is not only teaching what the Law says about outward behavior, but also about our internal motivation because the kingdom has come.)*

⊙ Choose a word that describes how you respond emotionally to this call to radical discipleship. *(Challenged, scared, uncertain, insecure, motivated, etc.)*

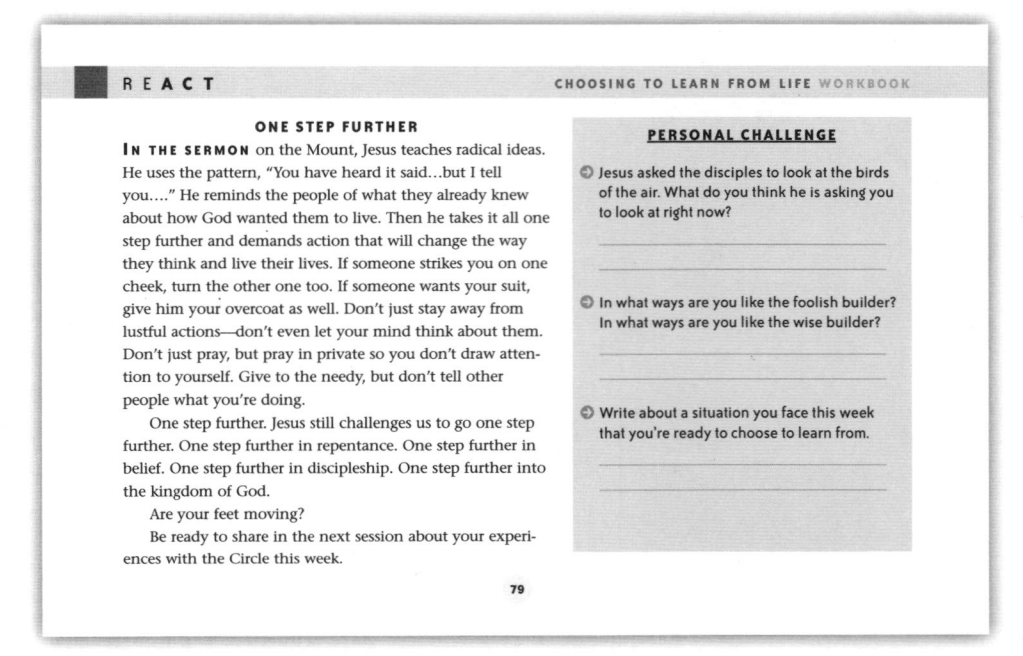

R E **A C T**   CHOOSING TO LEARN FROM LIFE WORKBOOK

ONE STEP FURTHER

IN THE SERMON on the Mount, Jesus teaches radical ideas. He uses the pattern, "You have heard it said...but I tell you...." He reminds the people of what they already knew about how God wanted them to live. Then he takes it all one step further and demands action that will change the way they think and live their lives. If someone strikes you on one cheek, turn the other one too. If someone wants your suit, give him your overcoat as well. Don't just stay away from lustful actions—don't even let your mind think about them. Don't just pray, but pray in private so you don't draw attention to yourself. Give to the needy, but don't tell other people what you're doing.

One step further. Jesus still challenges us to go one step further. One step further in repentance. One step further in belief. One step further in discipleship. One step further into the kingdom of God.

Are your feet moving?

Be ready to share in the next session about your experiences with the Circle this week.

79

PERSONAL CHALLENGE

⊙ Jesus asked the disciples to look at the birds of the air. What do you think he is asking you to look at right now?

_____

_____

⊙ In what ways are you like the foolish builder? In what ways are you like the wise builder?

_____

_____

⊙ Write about a situation you face this week that you're ready to choose to learn from.

_____

_____

As you wrap up your session, point out the "Personal Challenge" on page 79 of the participant workbook. Allow some quiet time for individuals to write personal answers. Ask members to share the personal challenges that they have set for themselves with at least one other person in the group.

Encourage participants to prepare for the next session by answering the "Thinking Ahead" questions at the beginning of Session 8.

Discuss how to support each other's plans for personal challenge. Close your session with prayer.

ONE STEP FURTHER

IN THE SERMON on the Mount, Jesus teaches radical ideas. He uses the pattern, "You have heard it said…but I tell you…." He reminds the people of what they already knew about how God wanted them to live. Then he takes it all one step further and demands action that will change the way they think and live their lives. If someone strikes you on one cheek, turn the other one too. If someone wants your suit, give him your overcoat as well. Don't just stay away from lustful actions—don't even let your mind think about them. Don't just pray, but pray in private so you don't draw attention to yourself. Give to the needy, but don't tell other people what you're doing.

One step further. Jesus still challenges us to go one step further. One step further in repentance. One step further in belief. One step further in discipleship. One step further into the kingdom of God.

Are your feet moving?

Be ready to share in the next session about your experiences with the Circle this week.

79

PERSONAL CHALLENGE

◉ Jesus asked the disciples to look at the birds of the air. What do you think he is asking you to look at right now?

_____

◉ In what ways are you like the foolish builder? In what ways are you like the wise builder?

_____

◉ Write about a situation you face this week that you're ready to choose to learn from.

_____

8 STILL LEARNING AFTER ALL THESE YEARS

You've explored all the steps of the Circle, you've seen how Jesus lived out the Circle in his life, and as your group completes this study, you'll be reminded that the process of learning and change never ends. God will use significant events all throughout your life to keep you humble and mindful of your faith. Opportunities to learn and grow are endless and the choice is simple: choose to ignore them or choose to learn from them. In light of the skills you have developed over these eight sessions, you now have the right tools to make that choice a little easier.

IN THIS SESSION, YOUR GROUP WILL:

Learn that discipleship is a Lifestyle of Learning

•

Explore opportunities to apply the Circle in everyday life

•

Discover that learning experiences come at unexpected times

•

Form a plan to become a life-long learner

PREPARATION:

- Read the Conclusion from *Choosing to Learn from Life.*
- Read Mark 1:15 and James 1:2
- If you are using *Choosing to Learn from Life Teaching DVD* or the *Learning Circle Slideshow* presentation, set up your equipment.
- Make sure you have Bibles to use in your session.
- Answer the discussion questions yourself so that you will have material for examples or prompting.

SCRIPTURAL BASIS:

- **James 1:2** — Regardless of how many *kairos* moments you have been through or how many times you have successfully moved through God's plan for change, your life remains a piece of clay which God can mold and shape. Trials are a part of life, and God can use all of them for our benefit, causing us to mature in our walk with him as we take each step closer toward his kingdom.

WELCOME YOUR GROUP members. As they come in, encourage them to review pages 81-82 Session 8 and answer the "Thinking Ahead" questions.

Begin with a brief review of last week's session. Invite participants to share some of the experiences they had with the Circle in the past week. Inspire them to dig a little deeper by sharing experiences that involved emotional and spiritual growth as opposed to the behavioral growth that most people tend to lean toward.

Then ask a volunteer to read aloud "Lifelong Learners" from the participant workbook, page 83.

LIFELONG LEARNERS

PEOPLE HAVE OFTEN said about *LifeShapes* that it's simple to understand, but difficult to do. Take heart, practice and failure are truly the ways that we become skilled and successful at doing anything. Do not expect to be just like Jesus after your first trip around the Circle. God gives us many opportunities, big and small, every day to work our way around the Circle. Ease yourself into it. Begin to grow and learn from the smaller moments and you will have trained yourself to prepare for the larger ones.

The Learning Circle really is the way that Jesus taught his disciples, both in the Sermon on the Mount and to all who would call themselves disciples today. In every *kairos* event you encounter, whether positive or negative, know that it is an opportunity for the kingdom of God to enter your life in a fresh way, for heaven to touch earth.

The process is one of repentance and faith. If that is the way that Jesus taught his first disciples, surely it's the way he continues to teach his disciples now, isn't it?

Take the Learning Circle into your workplace, your marriage, your friendships, your family life, your hurts and struggles, hopes and dreams. Jesus will always be the answer to your situation. The Circle is one tool to use as you dig for the presence of God in the landscape of your life. Remember, we are not achievers for Jesus, we are lifelong learners.

—from ***Choosing to Learn from Life,*** Conclusion

83

Use the questions on pages 84 of the participant workbook to break the ice and begin conversation among the group. Ask the group to share their answers to these questions. Your group has been together for an extended period of time; hopefully, they feel comfortable being open and honest in their time of sharing with each other. Encourage them to continue their honesty and vulnerability throughout this final session. Feel free to discuss only some of the questions as a group and encourage participants to explore the other questions on their own time.

Take a few minutes to answer these questions:

◎ Write about a recent time when your day turned out very differently than you expected.

◎ Identify some recent *kairos* moments: in your family, at work, in the community, at church, in a friendship, and so on.

◎ How many times have you been around the Circle in the last day? In the last week? In the last month?

84

IF YOU ARE using the DVD as part of your study, watch Chapter 6 now. Mike Breen tells the story "I've Got Just the Thing for You, Mr. Breen." If you are not using the DVD, read the abbreviated version that appears here.

I'VE GOT JUST THE THING FOR YOU, MR. BREEN.

I was on a flight from England to the States. I'd become well known as a preacher in Europe and was becoming well known as a teacher and preacher in America. People actually were prepared to pay for me to fly business class, and I did not feel called to turn that down.

I'd heard that there was a different culture in business class, more refined. Normally I dress quite casually, but I thought on this occasion I had better dress up like everybody else.

I went into the business class area of the plane, and it was immediately clear to everyone else that I'd never flown business class before. After take-off everyone settled into the flight. Some were reading while others caught up on work. Some watched movies and others tried to sleep. And then there was me. I was behaving like a five year-old in a toy store, playing with all the buttons and bells on the seat just to see what would happen when I pressed them!

After a while, I caught on. Everyone was trying to avoid all possible eye contact with this newbie!

After a fantastic lunch, I lay back in my seat until I was fully reclined and stretched out, thinking, This is the life! I wonder what it must be like in cattle class amongst all of those plebs.

A flight attendant asked me if I wanted a drink. I replied, "Sure, I'd like an orange juice, please." So she went to get me a large glass of orange juice. As she was walking toward me, for some unaccountable reason, she tripped.

The flight attendant was standing just next to me as she stumbled. Splat.

I leaped out of my seat. My fresh white shirt was dyed fresh orange; my pants were sticking to me.

The head flight attendant came over to me and said, "Mr. Breen, I've got just the thing for you. Club soda."

She returned with a very large bottle of club soda, about two liters worth.

"If you just go into the restroom there and put it on the orange, it will take the juice out."

So I crammed myself into an airplane restroom, held out my shirt, and poured on the soda.

At first I was quite amazed. Club soda really does take the color out. The orange was gone! But the mesmerizing moment of science passed when I realized that the miracle club soda was running right through my shirt and streaming down my chest.

I shuffled out of the bathroom to see the head flight attendant. Forgetting that on occasion I can have a rather loud voice and that this was not supposed to be one of those times, I said, "My underpants are wet."

By this stage, the whole cabin was in uproar just watching me.

As I shuffled along like a child uncomfortable in his diaper the head flight attendant said, "I've got just the thing for you, Mr. Breen." She gave me two towels. "It's a pressurized container, so you'll soon be dry. But the…er…dampish areas…you might wish to…use the towels on."

I attempted to do what she suggested, but it didn't really work. I returned to my seat rather gingerly. The guy seated next me turned and said, "Do you want a drink?"

I didn't think it was nearly as funny as he did.

"I've got just the thing for you, Mr. Breen."

There she was again. She said, "Mr. Breen, here's a fresh set of clothes for you. I think you'll need them."

I returned to the restroom to change. She had given me some gray sweat pants that were calf length. She had also given me an enormous orange (did I really need reminding?) golf shirt that was about knee length. I looked like Ronald Macdonald!

And that was the way that I traveled all the way across the Atlantic.

Well, that was a real opportunity for me to make some observations about myself. I was thinking things through and I made a new plan: Accept business class whenever anybody gives it to you. Be grateful, and just be the person God has created you to be.

In every *kairos* event you encounter, whether positive or negative, know that it is an opportunity for the kingdom of God to enter your life in a fresh way, for heaven to touch earth. Take the Learning Circle into your workplace, your marriage, your friendships, your family life, your hurts and struggles, hopes and dreams. Jesus will always be the answer to your situation. The Circle is one tool to use as you dig for the presence of God in the landscape of your life.

And don't worry if you find it difficult to work through the steps of the Circle. We are not achievers for Jesus; we are lifelong learners.

I am still learning after all these years.

After the story, ask a volunteer to read James 1:2. In light of this passage, discuss these questions as a group:

➲ Why is God certain to give us regular reminders of humility like the one he gave Mike Breen? *(To remind us that we are dependent on him for our own growth and spiritual maturity. To remind us of the qualities he wants us to have through his grace, not our own accomplishment.)*

➲ What is one lesson that you've been learning afresh after all these years?

You can supplement the DVD segment with the following material, or use this material independently. Be sure to allow time for Huddles in order to discuss the questions in the participant workbook and Going Deeper questions as appropriate.

→HUDDLES←

Whenever you see the Huddles icon, have your group break up into Huddles (groups of 2 or 3). Read the following paragraphs aloud; then give the Huddles a few minutes to discuss each question before moving on to the Going Deeper discussion questions. Your group may stay in their Huddles while you present material from each section.

(Prepare Slides 55–58). Display Slide 55. **Jesus taught his disciples in an intentional way. They saw the kingdom of God at work in his miracles and healings. They heard the authority with which he spoke about the kingdom of God. Jesus wanted to be sure they were connecting all the dots and coming up with a big picture of a life of discipleship. In the Sermon on the Mount, Jesus showed the disciples that the kingdom was near. Then he led them around the Circle through the process of repentance and faith.**

Slide 55

> **Observation.**
> **Reflection.**
> **Discussion.**
> **Planning.**
> **Accountability.**
> **Action.**

Slide 56

Display Slide 56. **Learning happens by events and process. This was the way Jesus taught the first disciples. We are his disciples, we are his learners. He has called us to a life of learning from him and then teaching others what we have learned. If we fail to learn (which includes change and growth) from him, we will fail in our call to make disciples out of others. The Learning Circle can be your tool; not just a tool for learning about the process of change, but a tool you can use to implement true change in your life.**

Just as Jesus wanted his first disciples to learn their way around the Circle, he wants you to learn your way around the Circle as well.

→HUDDLES← ➡ Which one of the six parts of the Circle has had the most impact on you? Explain. *(Be sure to share your own response as a leader. Be prepared to share first.)* ➡

The more times we go around the Circle, the more familiar we become with the process. *Display Slide 57.* We recognize *kairos* events more quickly. *Kairos* events allow us to enter a process of repentance and faith. We move more smoothly into the repentance process than we did before. Experience teaches us that while planning and accountability can be a little scary, we can succeed and have a positive result. While once we applied the Circle to the larger issues in our lives, now we see that we can apply it to the smaller things that happen to us, perhaps even on a daily basis. *Display Slide 58.* Having experienced a *kairos* event, we then begin the process of learning.

GOING DEEPER:

➡ How do you think understanding the Circle better is going to impact your life in the next few months? Consider all aspects of your life: behavioral, emotional, and spiritual.

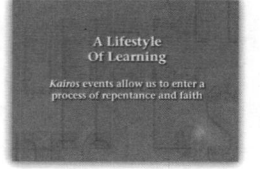

Slide 57

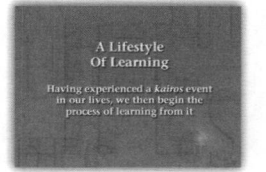

Slide 58

→HUDDLES← ◯ ➜ Has the Circle become easier for you as you've come to understand it more? Explain. *(Be sure to share your own response as a leader).* ➜

The Circle becomes a tool that we carry with us every day, everywhere we go, in every relationship, in every circumstance. It's the right tool, and we want to keep it within reach at all times. When we pull it out and use it, we see more and more of the kingdom of God—the rule of God in our lives, right now and right here.

→HUDDLES← ◯ ➜ How has studying the Learning Circle changed the way you look at ordinary events? *(Be sure to share your own response as a leader.)*

→HUDDLES← ◯ ➜ Has there been an extraordinary *kairos* event in your life to which you can go back and process through the Circle? This process may reveal some change in your life that God wanted but that you overlooked. ➜

GOING DEEPER:

➜ Which part of the Circle remains the hardest step for you to take?

GOING DEEPER:

➜ Name an event to which you have recently applied the Circle.

ASK SOMEONE TO read "The Extraordinary Ordinary" aloud from the participant workbook (page 88). Or, allow some quiet time for group members to read silently. Then discuss these questions as a group:

◉ Do you feel more like you're on the edge of taking the next step, like the Slinky, or more like you're tumbling down? Explain.

◉ How does the speed at which a Slinky moves remind you of discipleship? *(Sometimes it goes faster than we think it will. Sometimes it goes slower or even seems to stop.)*

R E A C T   CHOOSING TO LEARN FROM LIFE WORKBOOK

THE EXTRAORDINARY ORDINARY

REMEMBER THE SLINKY? We said that discipleship is like a Slinky. Life is a series of loops connected together by time as we go around and around the Circle.

One of the most fun things to do with a Slinky is to set it up so it will "walk" down a set of stairs. It's a mesmerizing experience. How does it do that? Sure, if we stop to analyze the physics of it, we could give a technical explanation of force and motion. But it's still cool to see! We set it up again and again to see if it will "walk" again.

You may feel at times as if you're going around and around the Circle and not moving forward. Perhaps you think you've learned that lesson enough times. Why doesn't God move on to something else? Or would it really be so bad just to walk a straight road for just a little while?

When you feel like that, remember the Slinky. It does move forward. The pace is not always steady. We watch while it seems to lean over the step precariously—and then it goes! Just when we think it's going to stop, it goes one more step. Discipleship is that way. It keeps going, even when we feel like the pace is slow. God is at work within us. His kingdom rules within us. He takes ordinary events and makes extraordinary learning occasions out of them. When you're inside the Circle, you can be sure you are moving forward!

88

As you wrap up your time together, point out the "Personal Challenge" on page 89 of the participant workbook. Allow some quiet time for individuals to write personal answers. Ask members to share the personal challenges they have set for themselves with at least one other person in the group.

Discuss how to support each other's plans for implementing these changes. Close your session with prayer and invite God to continue to teach you about the Circle as you take its principles with you into the world.

PERSONAL CHALLENGE

⊙ Name one lesson that God has taught you that was difficult for you to learn. What finally made the difference?

⊙ How do you feel about how fast your discipleship Slinky is moving at this point in your life? Explain.

⊙ Make a plan for how you will apply the Learning Circle in your life in a consistent way.

89

CONCLUSION: CHOOSING TO LEARN FROM LIFE LEADER'S GUIDE

You've just had your first glimpse into one aspect of Jesus' life that sets a precedent for how we should also live. Indeed, the Circle is simple to learn but difficult to follow—we often ignore opportunities in life to change because we just don't want to face the challenges involved. Be encouraged; start with those smaller kairos events and get used to the steps you have to take to get through them. As the Circle becomes more and more a part of your daily routine, you will discover that it begins to come naturally in all those significant moments.

As you have studied the *LifeShapes* Circle, many of your examples and those of your participants, have probably been focused on certain behaviors or attitudes that you want to change in your life. Changing the way we behave in our relationships, careers, or home life is usually only the first step. God wants to get into the deeper and hidden parts of our lives, he wants us to explore the true depths of who we are and why we are. The Circle has now equipped you with an excellent tool to help you in every part of your life. Don't be afraid to use it. God is looking for disciples who are authentic and transparent. That transparency happens in the context of a community that allows you to explore those moments when God challenges you to face the emotional and spiritual issues of your life. In this regard, you can truly become the spiritual being that God has designed you to be.

The depths of applications for the Circle are unending. You will use this tool for the rest of your life and still not experience all that it can show you. But that is the true nature of your life as a disciple of Christ. Be a life-long learner of all he has to show you!

Each *LifeShape* focuses on a certain aspect of Jesus' life. Every part of Jesus' life was lived out to the glory of God. As you take your journey in life, God desires that you strive to be like him in every way; to find a balance in every aspect, in every relationship, in every characteristic of your life. The journey does not end with the Circle, the Circle is only one of many things that God wants you to explore. You and your group may wish to continue the *LifeShapes* adventure with an in-depth study of the Semi-Circle. *Living in Rhythm with Life* will cut to the very heart of what our culture has taught us regarding the relationship between our work and our rest. Check out **www.LifeShapes.com** for more information and release dates. You will come away from this study feeling challenged to take that next step toward living a passionate life for Jesus.

The Word at Work
Around the World

What would you do if you wanted to share God's love with children on the streets of your city? That's the dilemma David C. Cook faced in 1870's Chicago. His answer was to create literature that would capture children's hearts.

Out of those humble beginnings grew a worldwide ministry that has used literature to proclaim God's love and disciple generation after generation. Cook Communications Ministries is committed to personal discipleship—to helping people of all ages learn God's Word, embrace his salvation, walk in his ways, and minister in his name.

● ●

Faith Kidz, RiverOak, Honor, Life Journey, Victor, NextGen . . . every time you purchase a book produced by Cook Communications Ministries, you not only meet a vital personal need in your life or in the life of someone you love, but you're also a part of ministering to José in Colombia, Humberto in Chile, Gousa in India, or Lidiane in Brazil. You help make it possible for a pastor in China, a child in Peru, or a mother in West Africa to enjoy a life-changing book. And because you helped, children and adults around the world are learning God's Word and walking in his ways.

Thank you for your partnership in helping to disciple the world. May God bless you with the power of his Word in your life.

For more information about our international ministries, visit www.ccmi.org.

A Passionate Life
Small Group Resource Kit by Mike Breen & Walt Kallestad

This Nine-Lessons *LifeShapes*™ course will help small groups break new discipleship ground. Through the DVD teachings, stimulating group and interpersonal discussion, and homework applications, groups are encouraged to stop doing discipleship, and to start living as authentic disciples of Jesus. Groups will learn how the basic shapes (Circle, Semi-Circle, Triangle, Square, etc.) of *LifeShapes* will help them recall and follow Jesus'example in every spiritual and personal aspect of their lives.

A Passionate Life Small Group Resource Kit
ISBN: 0-78144-279-6 • Item # 104443
1–Paperback edition of *A Passionate Life*
1–Leader's Guide
6–Workbooks
1–DVD-9 Teaching sessions with *LifeShapes*™ creator, Mike Breen

Additional Books, Leader's Guides and Workbooks available